THE
EIGHTIES

THE
EIGHTIES

Images of America

Vincent Virga

Foreword by Richard Rhodes

Edward Burlingame Books

An Imprint of HarperCollins*Publishers*

For Ed Burlingame and Kathy Banks

In Gratitude

ACKNOWLEDGMENTS

Thank you:

Nat Andriani	Joseph Montebello
Katherine Bang	Dianne Pinkowitz
Michael Beschloss	Michael Selleck
Ron Brenne	Jessica Shatan
Matthew Fink	Pat Skantze
Lester Glassner	Julianne Virga
Kim Lewis	Christa Weil
Bill Luckey	

HarperCollins books may be purchased for educational, business, or sales promotional use. For information, please write: Special Markets Department, HarperCollins Publishers, Inc., 10 East 53rd Street, New York, NY 10022.

FIRST EDITION

Library of Congress Cataloging-in-Publication Data

Virga, Vincent.
    The eighties : images of America / Vincent Virga ; foreword by Richard Rhodes. — 1st ed.
        p.   cm.
    ISBN 0-06-018206-7
    1. United States—History—1969–   —Pictorial works. 2. History, Modern—1945–   —Pictorial works. I. Title.
E839.V57   1992
973.927'022'2—dc20   90-56400

92 93 94 95 96 LP/EP 10 9 8 7 6 5 4 3 2 1

FOREWORD

RICHARD RHODES

pparently, gilded ages recur at hundred-year intervals, like noxious Brigadoons. Another one just went by. I culled a list from this book of the weird business the decade transacted: Disneyland in Tokyo, Star Wars, steroid-pumped women weight lifters, the war on drugs, Michael Jackson, Coke Classic, Jim and Tammy Faye Bakker, Chernobyl, recycling, the S&L scandal, rap, crack, pork rinds, quitting smoking, Iran-contra, the invasion of Grenada, the Islip garbage barge. And that's just a start, a bare minimum. "It is very difficult to predict," Niels Bohr remarked once, "especially the future." Who could have predicted the Eighties?

Vincent Virga, who's a novelist as well as the best picture editor I know, tries in the pages that follow to do something even more difficult: to predict, so to speak, the past. That's obscure. Let me take as my text a paragraph Lionel Trilling wrote somewhere that I've saved in my favorite-quotation file for years:

Some of the charm of the past consists of the quiet—the great distracting buzz of implication has stopped and we are left only with what has been fully phrased and precisely stated. And part of the melancholy of the past comes from our knowledge that the huge, unrecorded hum of implication was once there and left no trace—we feel that because it is evanescent it is especially human. We feel, too, that the truth of the great preserved monuments of the past does not fully appear without it. From letters and diaries, from the remote, unconscious corners of the great works themselves, we try to guess what the sound of the multifarious implication was and what it meant.

In some basic sense that mercifully escapes even deconstruction (the Eighties again!), the images that follow are primary. They're narrow slices across reality, frozen in time like a particle detector's record of a nuclear collision. They're irreducibly "true." But truth and meaning aren't necessarily the same thing (the laws of physics were around before we discovered them, for example), and what these images *mean* depends on how they're selected, compared, interpreted, and given context. (One of the jokes I remember from the Eighties: "She's so young she thinks Paul McCartney is someone who used to have a band called Wings.") In that sense what Virga does here corresponds to what historians do: he picks and chooses among the available evidence (in this case the huge *recorded* hum of implication) and arranges it so that it shows forth its meaning (or some of its many meanings). If he's done his work right—I think he has—he gives us a real past, reduced in density to the point where it makes some sense and we can bear it. You see: he predicts the past.

The image that comes to mind as the collective of all these images Virga has carefully assembled is the hologram. Because that special kind of photograph preserves so much information redundantly across its surface, you can tear it into small pieces and, looking into them and around the corner, as it were, see the entire original image, somewhat blurred. *The Eighties* is like that: an assemblage of scraps, to be sure, as all works of history are, but informed by such passionate, intelligent gathering that one may look through them and around their corners and see—remember, reexperience, relive—the decade.

A decade dark at the beginning, bright at the end. The decade of our Decline and Fall (ironic given the grandiose elaboration of our military power, "the greatest military buildup in peacetime in the history of the world") and the decade as well of historic, revolutionary change. Don't expect to find only sweetness and light here (courage, yes, especially in the faces of the men and women we valued and sometimes honored). Man-made death continued to be the primary scourge of the decade as of the century, checked by nuclear stalemate but a long way from coming under control. Restrained by the balance of terror from confronting the U.S.S.R. directly, we turned aside in wrath to assault our weakest neighbors in El Salvador and Nicaragua and poor little Grenada, just as the Soviets did in Afghanistan and Great Britain did in the Falklands. In the meantime the Japanese, who learned the bitter lesson of the self-destructiveness of war in World War II, devoted themselves to well-engineered consumer production. Mikhail Gorbachev and Ronald Reagan were the giants of the decade: painful reality confronting clever illusion. Despite the claims of zealots, neither side won the Cold War. Both sides spent themselves nearly into bankruptcy. While millions of children still die annually for want of simple inoculations, no one can claim victory, least of all moral victory.

If man-made death haunted the Eighties, Virga makes the happy discovery that Eighties people improvised a therapy for it: naming the dead. Those who would let us die of indifference and neglect, those who would murder us, require for the numbing of their consciences that our deaths go unrecorded. Naming the dead denies them that evasion. The dead rise up again to insist on meaning. Thus Maya Ying Lin's brilliant, compassionate Vietnam Veterans Memorial wall in Washington, D.C., which reflects the presence of the mourners who stand or kneel before it and allows them to enter into its obsidian depths, to join with the 57,939 names at least of the loved ones they lost. Thus the Names Project, a collection of named and decorated quilts to honor the men and women lost to AIDS, the collection silently and tragically enlarging its ground as the years go by. Thus the book of the disappeared of El Salvador, precious photographs, all the bereaved have left except for the odds and ends of bones exhumed by volunteer forensic archaeologists.

It seems to me that the United States succumbed to a postfascist mentality in the Eighties, with a national leadership manipulated by some of the nastiest people around, contemptuous people who thought it was cute to appoint federal administrators to gut the agencies they were supposed to manage. I heard people I'd thought respectable using words like "nigger" and "kike" again. They dared to do so because they felt permission trickling down from the top, and it was. The Eighties were the years when we spent billions on a weapons boondoggle right off of a Steven Spielberg backlot while a million American children went homeless, when feral entrepreneurs savaged our savings and loans, when famine became a political decision rather than a natural phenomenon, when fear that others might enjoy choices that the fearful had been forbidden converged on abortion (woe betide us when our national leaders begin celebrating "family values," the way the Nazis used to do). Lee Iacocca's Chrysler Corporation went on welfare in the Eighties, and Iacocca shifted the blame to the Japanese. Charles Keating, impresario of thrift and arch enemy of porn, picked our pockets for $2.5 billion, which is what it cost over the years to build the interstate highway system. Swaggart wept. Farmers struggled through the worst decade of their lives as property values declined and banks called their loans (and dropped depositors' funds into glamorous black holes like Michael Milken's junk bonds). Ed Meese played the Sheriff of Nottingham, Ollie North the Unknown Soldier. We tilted toward Iraq and welcomed Saddam Hussein, fresh from mustard-gassing Kurds and Iranians, as our ally. John Lennon was murdered; so was Anwar Sadat. Alexander Haig found himself, as he told us from the White House, briefly and uncharacteristically "in control." Chernobyl and Bophal revealed the corruption of unchecked authority working in secret. It all comes together—Virga's keen, unblinking eye—in the gathering of the decade's two indistinguishable first families, one in the White House and one on television, each led by a present or former Ronald Reagan wife ("I'll never vote for that man," said a grandmother I knew who lived in St. Joseph, Missouri, Reagan's first wife's hometown, "not after what he did to that nice Jane Wyman").

Not to be morbid. There was more to life, even in the Eighties, than corruption. Street artists in New York had been evolving the best graffiti since ancient Rome; in the Eighties it went full color. Salsa surpassed catsup as the nation's leading condiment. Bungee-jumping went commercial. In the right circles you could go for weeks without encountering cigarette smoke (the new aggressive stink was perfume, artificial and hyperodiferous, laved on, it seemed, by the gallon). Yuppies came along to amuse us. (A resident of Rowe, Massachusetts, commenting in the *New York Times* about out-of-towners marching through his village protesting the local nuclear power plant: "I call it yuppie panic. They're people who want you to quit smoking and eat tofu.") Personal computers and compact disks introduced us to the abundance of digital processing. Martin Luther King Day became a national holiday. *Voyager* carried us out to tour our brother and sister planets: don't you wish Earth had planetary rings? Both my kids finished college and started in respectable (salaried!) professions—yours too, I hope.

I visited the Berlin Wall two weeks after it was breached and watched East Germans crowding through the gap to West Berlin, where they wandered the shopping malls stunned by the lights and the luxury. A whole continent of people behaved as if they'd just been released from forty years in jail, and they had. They were released to face the problems the Communist regimes that ran the jails had barricaded off since 1945—problems of economics and nationalist fury, problems we'll be living with for decades to come—but at least they could choose in the light of day.

The twentieth will be remembered as the bloodiest of all the centuries in the history of the world—100 million, maybe 120 million, dead by violence—but the Eighties marked the turning of that dark tide. Implicit in the discovery of how to release nuclear energy was the certainty that the new knowledge would force human beings to adjust their political relationships to avoid world-scale war or see their civilization destroyed. The adjustment came tacitly in the 1960s, after the Cuban Missile Crisis, when the United States and the U.S.S.R. quietly found ways to accommodate each other short of armed conflict. In the Eighties Mikhail Gorbachev—certainly one of the great moral and political leaders of our time or of any time—made the change explicit and probably permanent. Much as I despise the corruption of the decade, particularly the ascendancy in the United States of contemptuous and murderous wealth (we have had no more brutally violent a President than George Bush), on the larger scale of history the Eighties was a triumph for human freedom.

And so the Statue of Liberty appears and reappears through this fascinating book, enigmatic as the Sphinx, standing for something that people in places like Tiananmen Square believed to be worth dying for, something that we who own the copyright on the great lady hardly seem to believe anymore. I like the notion of Liberty renovated for her birthday in this decade that saw liberty renovated across great stretches of the globe. Isn't it time we renovated her spirit here at home?

1

6

5

FIRST

2

FAMILIES

3

4

1980

· *Who's Kiddin' Who?* ·

1

CHARLIE CHAPLIN, PAULETTE GODDARD

2

...DIANE KEATON, WOODY ALLEN

3

ENRICO CARUSO

4

...LUCIANO PAVAROTTI

5

6

ABC News opened its evening broadcast on the first day
of the decade with the greeting it would use for another
385 days. It was the 59th day of the hostage crisis.

7

8

2

9

Left, Russian soldiers and Afghani children

Less than a year after the Ayatollah Khomeini ousted the American-backed Shah from Iran, the U.S.S.R. invaded Afghanistan to protect its southern border from Khomeini's fundamentalists. President Carter said, "We hope to persuade the Soviets that a country cannot impose its system of society on another."

10

13

12

·Women in Uniform·

14

"A beauty pageant is…the biggest source of scholarship money for women.… You parade around for men in order to get to college." —Gloria Steinem

"We do not want our daughters treated like men or like sex playmates in the armed forces."—Phyllis Schlafly. Below, her anti-ERA supporters greet Senator Jesse Helms (Schlafly is at right).

"We've misread the market today. We're not as well prepared for it as we should be, and we're late. It's a big mistake."
—Henry Ford II

The Dream Endures: Eighty thousand Cambodians and other Asians crowded refugee camps in Thailand...

...and 100,000 Cubans crossed the Straits of Florida to the United States.

18

19

Mano Blanco, the calling card of the death squads

Roberto D'Aubuisson

El Playon

23

Roberto D'Aubuisson, holding posts in Salvadoran intelligence, the ARENA coalition, and the National Guard, inherits CIA files (set up under President Kennedy) on suspected Salvadoran leftists. People start to disappear. In a country of 5.3 million, 8,400 were killed in 1980; one for every square mile.

1980

25

24

26

On its southernmost coast, America's melting pot comes to a boil. When an all-white jury exonerated a group of Dade County police in the death of Arthur McDuffie, the black community erupted in the worst violence since the Detroit riots of 1967. Cubans detained by the U.S. Immigration Service (below) rioted for their own reasons.

"The free enterprise system is clearly outlined in the Book of Proverbs."—Jerry Falwell, spokesperson for the Moral Majority

George Bush labeled Ronald Reagan's strategies "voodoo economics" until he joined the ticket as Vice President.

Amy Carter and family celebrate President Carter's renomination. His rise in opinion polls during the hostage crisis knocked the problematic Ted Kennedy (top) out of the running.

Masaya, Nicaragua (left): After the overthrow of dictator Anastasio Somoza, 10,000 jubilant supporters mobbed a victorious Daniel Ortega. Southern Iraq (right): When Saddam Hussein invaded Iran, a relieved United States supplied him with intelligence and heavy weapons.

36

37

Gdansk shipyard: Union leader Lech Walesa during the general strike that gave rise to Poland's Solidarity union.

38

39

Operation Eagle Claw: The administration's attempt to rescue the hostages from Iran ended in disaster. Carter plummeted in the polls.

40

41

BROKEN
PROMISES

"...a sort of
supreme anchor-
man..."
—Donald T. Regan

DECAY

"These are the new icons of beauty...

Calvin Klein Underwear

43

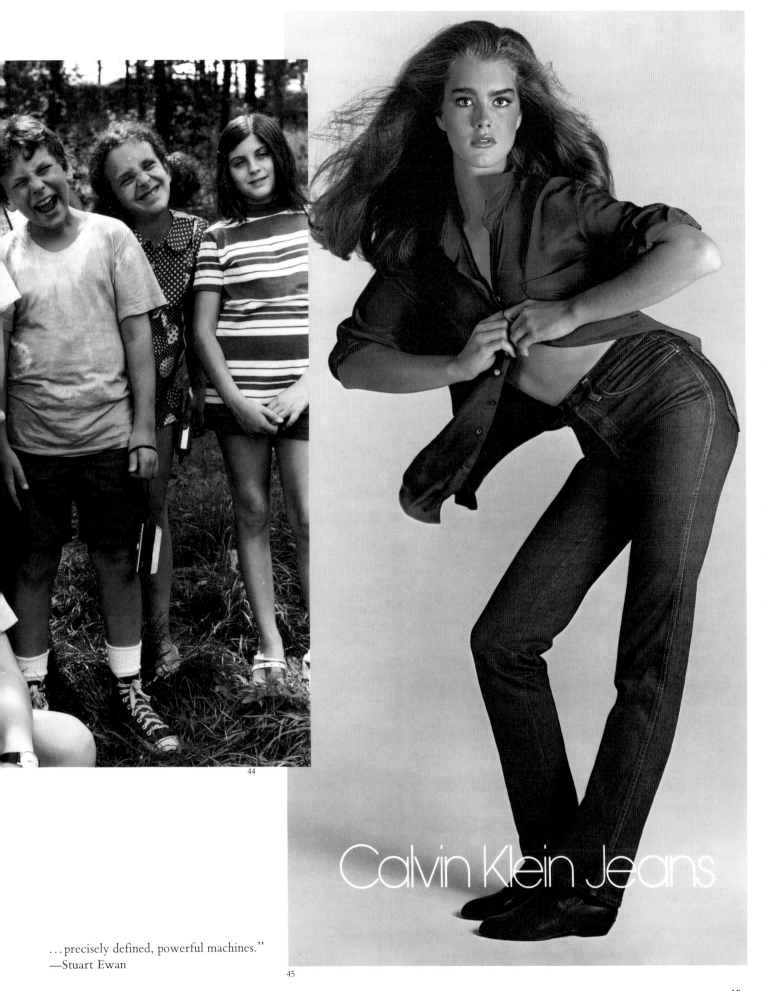

44

45

...precisely defined, powerful machines.''
—Stuart Ewan

Calvin Klein Jeans

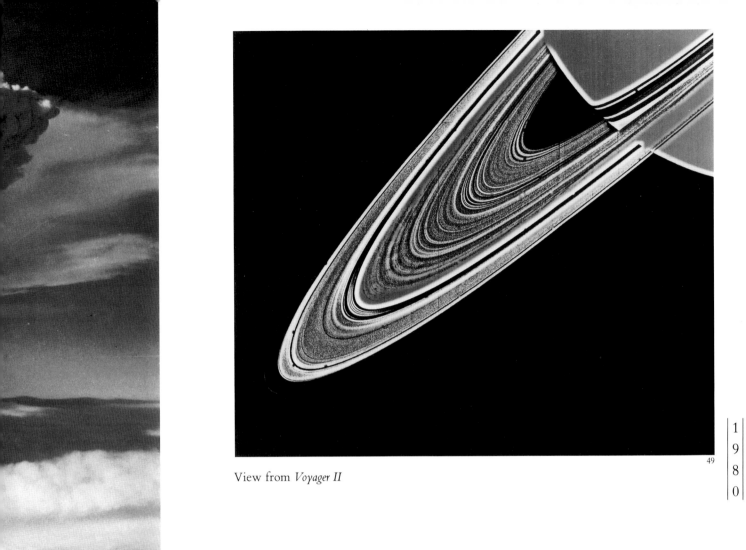

View from *Voyager II*

49

48

Mt. St. Helens, Washington state

Vigil for Lennon...

Vigil for Wenz, Kroenig

Killed by Gunfire: John Lennon, Jiog Wenz, and Vernon Kroenig. This page, Dorothy Kazel, Ita Ford, Maura Clarke, and Jean Donovan— three American nuns and one Catholic lay worker—ambushed by the Salvadoran National Guard.

52

"We know that in the blood of the martyrs who lie here is the spirit of liberty."
—Rev. David Rodriquez, Salvadoran priest

53

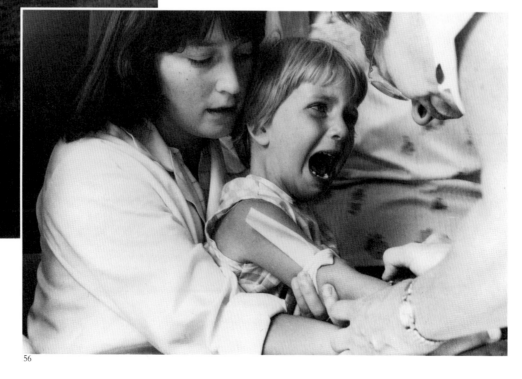

55

Dolphins trapped by commercial tuna fishers (above) stirred up a lunch-box ban that was the most successful consumer boycott ever. Below, an evacuated Love Canal child gets a blood test.

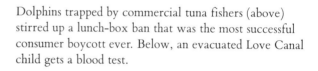

DIVERSIONS

Left to right from top: Former U.S. Rep. Michael Myers caught in the act; Judy Chicago's *Dinner Party*; James Schuyler, Pulitzer poet; birth of CNN; Sagan: *Cosmos*; Hawn: *Private Benjamin*; Parton, Fonda, and Tomlin: *9 to 5*; De Niro: *Raging Bull*; Chamberlain: *Shogun*; Eric Heiden; Redgrave: *Playing for Time*; Hagman: Who shot J.R.?

1
9
8
0

Farewell: Gordie Howe, Muhammad Ali, Beverly Sills retire

DOROTHY DAY, b. 1897 [72]

Social activist

WILLIAM O. DOUGLAS, b. 1898 [73]

Supreme Court justice

JIMMY DURANTE, b. 1893 [74]

Entertainer

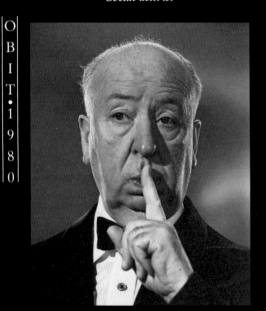

ALFRED HITCHCOCK, b. 1899 [75]

Film director

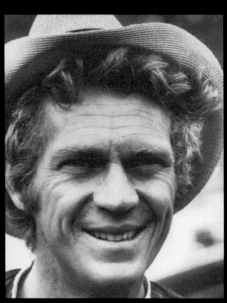

STEVE McQUEEN, b. 1930 [76]

Actor

GEORGE MEANY, b. 1894 [77]

Union president

JESSE OWENS, b. 1913

Athlete

[78]

MOHAMMED RIZA SHAH PAHLEVI
b. 1919

Shah of Iran

JEAN PIAGET, b. 1896

Child psychologist

ARCHBISHOP OSCAR ROMERO
b. 1917

Liberation theologian

JEAN-PAUL SARTRE, b. 1905

Philosopher and writer

PETER SELLERS, b. 1925

Actor

TITO, b. 1892

Politician

MAE WEST, b. 1892

Actress and dramatist

1981

· Who's Kiddin' Who? ·

TEDDY ROOSEVELT

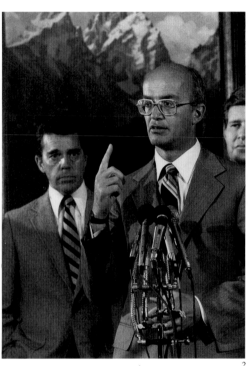

...JAMES WATT

FIORELLO LA GUARDIA

...ED KOCH

"Thank goodness it's back—that froth in the confection of language, that lovely whipped-cream of a word—luxury."
—New York Times Magazine

Former hostage greeted by a joyful nation. "The most emotional experience of our lives!"—George Bush, Vice President elect

Right, top, Congress tried to tie U.S. aid for the Salvadoran government to human rights reforms, but the new administration saw the rebellion as a textbook case of Communist aggression fomented by nearby Nicaragua, and dispatched fifty-six Green Beret advisers to the scene. Below, Salvadoran government troops claim a victory against the rebels.

7

9

10

11

12

13

Washington, D.C., March 30 (left); St. Peter's Square, Rome, May 13 (above). Cairo, October 6 (below), rebel forces in his own army succeeded in killing Anwar Sadat.

14

15

16

Ottawa, Canada (top left): A recovered
Ronald Reagan at his first international sum-
mit. Tonopah, Nevada (left) (live population
2,200): Site for a proposed $30 billion "dense
pack" arrangement of MX-ICBMs. Damas-
cus (above): Terrorists take 103 hostages at
the airport. *Time* dubbed 1981 the "Year of
Terrorism."

Lady Diana Spencer

Mu'ammar Qaddafi

20

Jean Harris (above)

21

Sandra Day O'Connor (back row, far right)

DIVERSIONS

Left to right from top: A restored Gance *Napoleon*; Bergen, Bisset: *Rich and Famous*; Mel Gibson: *Gallipoli*; "Hill Street Blues"; Lena Horne on Broadway; Ford: *Indiana Jones*; Williamson: *Excalibur*; Miss Piggy; Dunaway: *Mommie Dearest*; Christopher Reeve; Selleck: "Magnum, P.I."; a reunited Garfunkel and Simon

Rubik's Cube

Women choose women doctors.

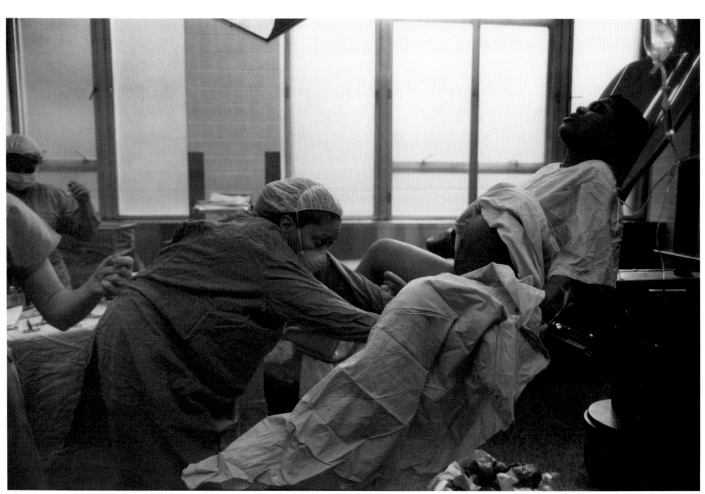

36

• *Men Out of Uniform* •

37

*"The life of a city
begins and ends in the street."*
—ROBERTA BRANDEIS GRATZ

38

Guardian Angels, NYC

1
9
8
1

41

BARYSHNIKOV

44

BIRD

42

43

WINFIELD

1
9
8
1

47

46

NAVRATILOVA

45

MONTANA

48

49

50

Jane Fonda's Work Out catches on.

48

California: The medfly crisis creates turmoil over the use of pesticides in agriculture.

Mature form

It was called the "gay cancer" or GRID: Gay Related Immune Deficiency. The retrovirus believed to be implicated in this new disease would not be isolated for another two years.

Budding particles

Union busting: Before the year ends, Lech Walesa is arrested, martial law is declared, and Poland's new trade unions are suspended. In the United States, when 11,600 air traffic controllers continue their strike, the President fires them.

1981

Miami Beach: Thirty-three Haitians drown fleeing Baby Doc Duvalier's regime.

Madrid: On Picasso's hundredth birthday, after spending decades in New York as a protest against Franco, *Guernica* goes home.

ROGER NASH BALDWIN, b. 1884 [57]

ACLU founder

KARL BÖHM, b. 1894 [58]

Conductor

OMAR BRADLEY, b. 1893 [59]

General, U.S. Army

PADDY CHAYEFSKY, b. 1923 [60]

Writer

MOSHE DAYAN, b. 1915 [61]

Chief of Staff, Israeli Defense Forces

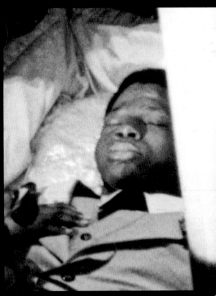

MICHAEL A. DONALD, b. 1961 [62]

KKK victim

GLORIA GRAHAME, b. 1924 63

Actress

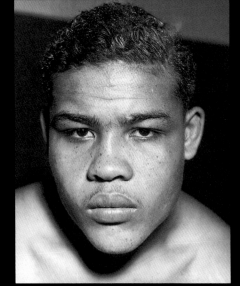

JOE LOUIS, b. 1914 64

Athlete

ALBERT SPEER, b. 1905 65

Hitler's architect

ROY WILKINS, b. 1901 66

Civil rights activist

NATALIE WOOD, b. 1938 67

Actress

WILLIAM WYLER, b. 1902 68

Film director

AIDS death toll: 163

1982

· Who's Kiddin' Who? ·

BARBARA STANWYCK

...MERYL STREEP

AGATHA CHRISTIE

...P.D. JAMES

Above, malling (from Valspeak, "to hang out"). Below, Pac-Man (from Japanese *paku*, "to eat").

Nicaragua: Since the Boland Amendment made it illegal to use CIA or Defense Department funds to overthrow the Nicaraguan government, William Casey (right) helped the Reagan administration find creative ways to supply a contra army with military aid.

The Philippine Republic: Ferdinand Marcos receives U.S. token of friendship.

El Salvador: With the United States presumably stopping Nicaraguan supply lines to rebel forces, the Salvadoran government promises open elections. "Vote in the morning, die in the afternoon" becomes a popular street slogan.

7

10

9

11

Amid growing concern over acid rain, clean air standards were relaxed to "a more reasonable pace." Preservation of historical buildings (center) continued. In the Brazilian rainforest (far right), a tree is marked for cutting.

12

13

*"We have altered the composition of the delicate
medium that is our home in space."*

—LOUISE B. YOUNG

14

State of Maine. Nearly every state in the union was dealing with the highest unemployment since 1945.

15

18

Three states short of ratification, ERA fails.
Eleanor Smeal, president of NOW, says,
"The campaign is not over."

20

Demonstration in Ann Arbor, Michigan

. . . Banned books

21

2,075 brides and 2,075 grooms are united by the Reverend Moon.

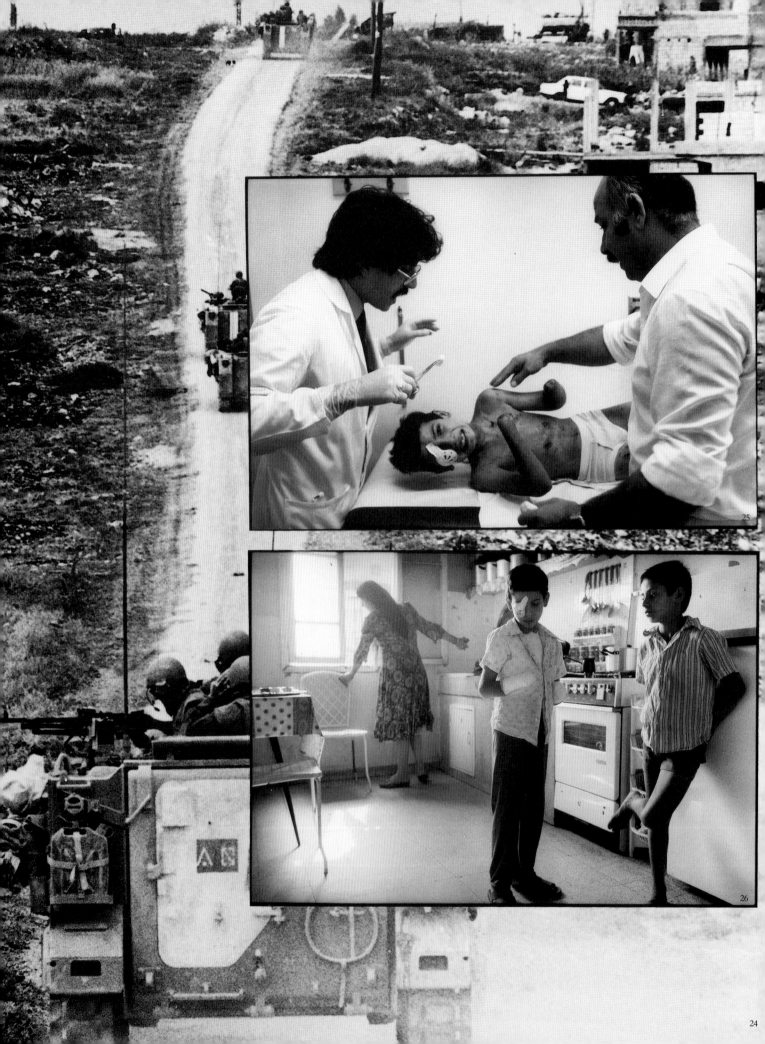

1
9
8
2

Israel invades West Beirut, and President Reagan sends in the Marines, assuring Congress there is no danger, just a need to prevent reprisals. But 700 to 800 Palestinian refugees die while under the guard of militant Lebanese Christians, Israel's allies.

Project Orbis: Surgeons in a flying operating room travel the world on sight-saving missions. Below, the Pet-a-Pet program successfully reaches out to the elderly and mentally handicapped.

1
9
8
2

29

30

DIVERSIONS

From top, left to right: Andrews, Irons: "Brideshead Revisited"; Coppola directing Kinski, Woods: *One from the Heart*; Spacek, Lemmon: *Missing*; *E.T.;* Tom Watson; William Westmoreland sues CBS; Hoffman: *Tootsie*; Zech: *Veronika Voss*; Ralph Waldo Emerson (1803-1882); Ford: *Blade Runner*; El Salvador's President Duarte

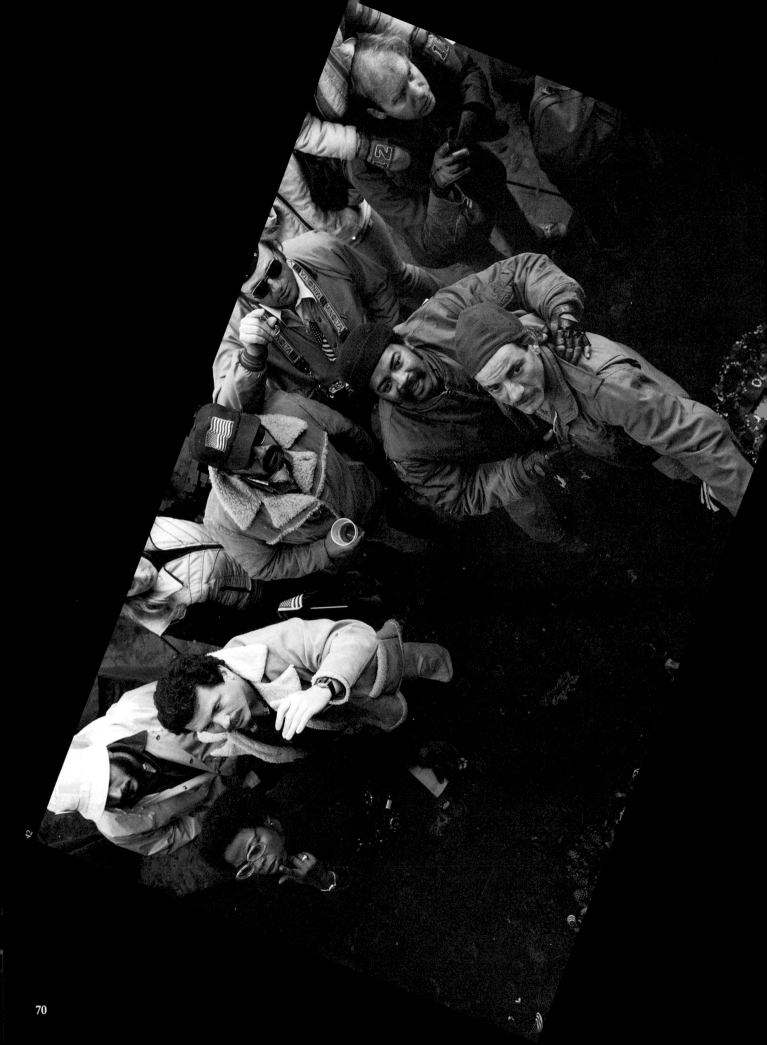

Washington, D.C.:
Designed by Maya
Ying Lin and dedi-
cated November 13,
the powerfully moving
Vietnam Veterans
Memorial draws
unprecedented
numbers of visitors.

JOHN BELUSHI, b. 1949 45
Actor

INGRID BERGMAN, b. 1915 46
Actress

LEONID BREZHNEV, b. 1906 47
Communist Party leader

JOHN CHEEVER, b. 1912 48
Writer

DAVID DUBINSKY, b. 1892 49
Labor leader

**RAINER WERNER FASSBINDER
b. 1946** 5
Film director

51

HENRY FONDA, b. 1905 52
Actor

GLENN GOULD, b. 1932 5
Musician

PAULA PRINCE, *one of eight victims of poisoned Tylenol*

O B I T • 1 9 8 2

CELIA JOHNSON, b. 1908   54
Actress

GRACE KELLY, b. 1929   55
Actress

ARCHIBALD MACLEISH
b. 1892   56
Writer

THELONIOUS MONK, b. 1920   57
Musician

ELEANOR POWELL, b. 1912   58
Actress

AYN RAND, b. 1905   59
Writer

ARTHUR RUBINSTEIN, b. 1887   60

LEE STRASBERG, b. 1899   61

KING VIDOR, b. 1896   62

1983

·Who's Kiddin' Who?·

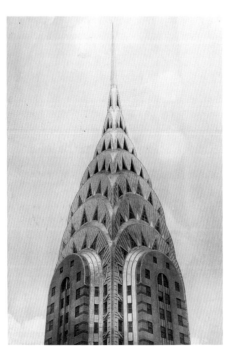

GEORGE GERSHWIN

...ANDREW LLOYD WEBER

CHRYSLER BUILDING

...AT&T BUILDING

5

Candlelight vigil, Washington, D.C. The Pasteur Institute in Paris isolates the virus; in the United
States, the Centers for Disease Control, recognizing that GRID is not just a "gay disease,"
renames it Acquired Immune Deficiency Syndrome. "Federal officials consider it an epidemic,
yet you rarely hear a thing about it." —Dan Rather, on the "CBS Evening News"

8

Lee Iacocca (above) sells Chrysler's tank division and reports a profit.

Between 1981 and 1985 the national debt climbs from $58 billion to $200 billion. "No one really understands what's going on with all these numbers." —Budget Director David Stockman (left)

PACs (left) spend an estimated $1.5 billion a year. "When these political action committees give money, they expect something in return other than good government." —Sen. Robert Dole

"Business as usual will not be accepted by the people." A stirring grassroots campaign elected Harold Washington (below) Chicago's first African-American mayor.

1
9
8
3

FOR LEASE
INDUSTRIAL
PROPERTY
5 ACRES · 20,000 Sq. Ft. Bldg.
681-0754 · Zoned M3 · 521-4257

10

The steel industry begins the long climb back. Though only 29 percent of America's steel mills were active in 1980,
a trimmer industry had 90 percent back in operation by 1989.

Right, between 1981 and 1984
20,000 farms are auctioned off.
Farmers, once 25 percent of the
population in the 1930s,
dwindled to 3 percent.

In Smyrna, Tennessee, "Rosie the Riveter" works for Honda.

13

14

"Star Wars," *Star Wars*

15

Korean Air Lines flight 007 is shot down by a Soviet fighter jet.

Military hardware, Nicaragua

Speak softly: With Congress forbidding direct attempts to overthrow Nicaragua's government, the Reagan administration stages a massive training exercise in neighboring Honduras called "Operation Big Pine."

18

Self-defense for women: "Take Back the Night"

U.S. Marine command post, Beirut, October 25

Grenada, three days later

20

21

College students play Trivial Pursuit on the world's largest game board.

22

The owner of a supermarket chain bought Murillo's *The Last Supper* and hung it in Pasadena, Texas.

DIVERSIONS

From top, left to right: Lee Krasner; Sally Quinn: first woman in space; Pacino: *Scarface*; Bando Tamasaburo V; Dillon, Rourke: *Rumble Fish*; Fassbinder's *Berlin Alexandreplatz*; Alice Walker; return of *Vertigo*, rereleased after twenty-five years; Bette Midler; Boy George; last episode of "M*A*S*H"; first Chinese *Death of a Salesman*; nuclear plant shutdowns; *A Chorus Line* breaks the Broadway record for consecutive performances

GEORGE BALANCHINE, b. 1904 [37]

Choreographer

EUBIE BLAKE, b. 1883 [38]

Composer

PAUL ''BEAR'' BRYANT, b. 1913 [39]

Athletic coach

LUIS BUÑUEL, b. 1900 [40]

Film director

GEORGE CUKOR, b. 1899 [41]

Film director

WILLIAM HARRISON ''JACK''
DEMPSEY, b. 1895

Athlete

AIDS death toll: 2,081

LYNN FONTANNE, b. 1887 [43]

Actress

BUCKMINSTER FULLER, b. 1895 [44]

Architect and philosopher

IRA GERSHWIN, b. 1896 [45]

Lyricist

HARRY JAMES, b. 1916 [46]

Musician

RALPH RICHARDSON, b. 1902 [47]

Actor

GLORIA SWANSON, b. 1899 [48]

Actress

JAMES A. J. VAN DER ZEE
b. 1886 [49]

Photographer

REBECCA WEST, b. 1892 [50]

Writer

TENNESSEE WILLIAMS, b. 1911 [51]

Writer

1984

· Who's Kiddin' Who? ·

PETER BROOK

...STEVEN BERKOFF

LUCHINO VISCONTI

...FRANCO ZEFFIRELLI

First free walk in space

POLITICIANS

6

With the death of Soviet leader Yuri Andropov, Konstantin
Chernenko (front right) comes into power. Watch that man on
the left.

Jesse Jackson and the Rainbow
Coalition

7

Gary Hart: "If anyone wants to
put a tail on me, go ahead."

8

New York Senator Alfonse
D'Amato and President
Ronald Reagan

95

9

Leaving Lebanon

10

GIVE ME LIBERTY FROM NUCLEAR WEAPONS STOP TESTING GREENPEACE

Lee Iacocca raises $30 million to renovate the Statue of Liberty.

Opposite, besieged vice presidential candidate Geraldine Ferraro tells reporters, "The American people have a right to know whether I'm married to Jack the Ripper." Top, New York Governor Mario Cuomo's keynote speech is a hit. "At his best, he can orchestrate these sessions with a wit and bravura to match John Kennedy's." —Garry Wills

14

Elizabeth Holtzman, Betty Friedan, Bella Abzug

15

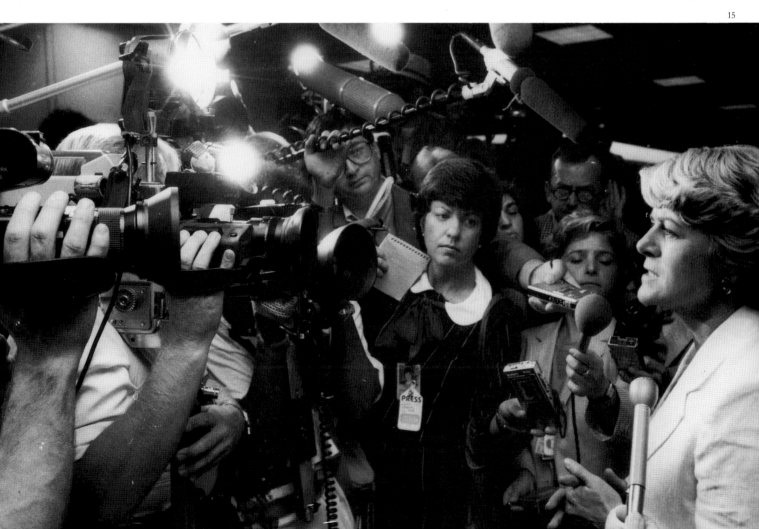

16

Economic growth, at 6.8 percent, is the highest since 1951. President Reagan remarked in an interview that many homeless were "homeless, you might say, by choice."

17

"A man totally without guile, operating in a world of cunning rascals...a stubborn dreamer,
a radical reformer...." —*Time*

Water polo team coach Monte Nitzkowski (left) and Captain Terry Schroeder with the team's bestselling pin-up poster

Above, Greg Louganis, and the entire diving team: (front row from left) McCormick, Seufert, Wyland, Mitchell, Louganis; (back row from left) Merriott, Kimball

MARY T. MEAGHER   23

VALERIE BRISCO–HOOKS   24

EVELYN ASHFORD   25

CARL LEWIS   26

MARY LOU RETTON   27

JOAN BENOIT   28

1
9
8
4

Team
gold:
Men's
gymnastics

22

JEFFREY BLATNICK   29

30

31

South African Commute

32

Bhopal

33

34

Pro-lifers bomb a
Florida Planned
Parenthood clinic
and call it a "gift
to Jesus on His
birthday."

35

36

Wiseguy Tommaso Buscetti, a key informant in the "pizza connection,"
breaks *omerta*, the code of silence, complaining that the "honored asso-
ciation" had been replaced by "a bunch of assassins." As the decade
progressed, the mob began to look like a thing of the past.

37

DIVERSIONS

Mud wrestlers; Julius Erving and Kareem Abdul-Jabbar;
Nancy and Ron in Hawaii

38

39

From top left, left to right:
Victoria de los Angeles on CD;
FedEx arrives; Hunt: *Year of
Living Dangerously*; Christmas
with "Dynasty"; Davis: *A
Passage to India*; Gless, Daly:
"Cagney and Lacey"; Stock-
well, Stanton: *Paris, Texas*;
Bridges: *Starman*

HAPPY BIRTHDAY
1934   1984
DONALD DUCK

ANSEL ADAMS, b. 1902 49
Photographer

COUNT BASIE, b. 1904 50
Musician

RICHARD BURTON, b. 1925 51
Actor

TRUMAN CAPOTE, b. 1924 52
Writer

GENERAL MARK CLARK, b. 1896 53
Soldier

MICHEL FOUCAULT, b. 1926 54
Philosopher

INDIRA GANDHI, b. 1917 55
Prime minister of India

JANET GAYNOR, b. 1906 56
Actress

TITO GOBBI, b. 1915 57
Singer

Lillian Hellman, b. 1907 [58]
Writer

Alfred A. Knopf, b. 1892 [59]
Publisher

Raymond Kroc, b. 1902 [60]
Entrepreneur

James Mason, b. 1909 [61]
Actor

Mabel Mercer, b. 1900 [62]
Singer

Ethel Merman, b. 1909 [63]
Singer and actress

François Truffaut, b. 1932 [64]
Film director

Johnny Weissmuller, b. 1904 [65]
Athlete and actor

AIDS death toll: 5,440

O B I T • 1 9 8 4

111

1985

·*Who's Kiddin' Who?*·

LEONTYNE PRICE

...KIRI TI KANAWA

J. D. SALINGER

...JAY MCINERNEY

All present and accounted for: Amid domestic protest over U.S. policies toward Nicaragua's Sandinista government, Congress cut off all forms of aid to the contra rebels late in 1984. That year the U.S. government mined Nicaragua's harbors with firecracker bombs, and a CIA manual turned up instructing the contras in the "neutralization" of leftists. In 1985 the Reagan administration goes on to embargo trade and veto a World Bank loan to the Sandinistas. Stateside protest grows. Then Daniel Ortega goes to Moscow seeking aid, photos of his visit show up in U.S. newspapers, and Congress flip-flops, authorizing $27 million in "humanitarian aid" for the contra movement. Secretary of State George Shultz (second from right) pays a call on President Ortega to assure him of our good intentions.

6

7

Nouvelle Society: Steinbergs, Trump, and van Gogh. "I look for things for the art sake, and the beauty sake, and the deal sake." —Donald Trump

8

Young urban professionals, day

Young urban professionals, night

When the going gets tough, the tough go shopping.

13

When S&Ls were deregulated in 1980, assets were valued at $32.2 billion. Two years later, they were worth $3.7 billion. Three years after that, the news began to break.

American farmers carry
crosses for friends
who committed suicide.

1985

14

15

Wildlife preserve, China

Bitburg, West Germany

"Some of us are like a shovel brigade that follows a parade down Main Street."
—Donald Regan

17

19

Greenpeace's *Rainbow Warrior* scuttled
by French covert operators

MOVE headquarters in Philadelphia
leveled by the police

20

Gay-bashing victim testifies

Rome airport attacked by the PLO

Ferdinand Marcos forbade farmers on the Island of Negros to grow crops other than sugar cane. When the sugar industry collapsed, fields went fallow and residents went hungry.

23

24

1
9
8
5

ETHIOPIA

In the United States, the hungry line up for free cheese.

"We Are the World": "Good morning, children of the '80s. This is your Woodstock, and it's long overdue." —Joan Baez. Left, organizer Bob Geldof (center) is shown with David Bowie (left), Paul McCartney, and Peter Townsend. Tina Turner and Mick Jagger (below) are among other performers at a Live Aid benefit.

27

28

1985

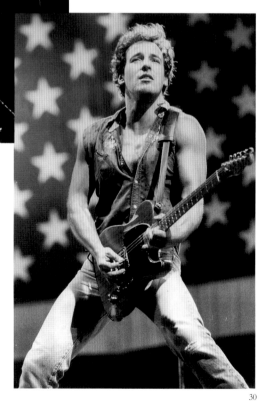

Cyndi Lauper, "Girls Just Want to Have Fun"

29

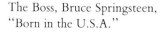

The Boss, Bruce Springsteen, "Born in the U.S.A."

30

Michael Jackson, "Thriller"

31

Fiftieth anniversary: "Alcoholics Anonymous is a fellowship of men and women who share their experience, strength, and hope with one another...."

32

34

When Rock Hudson, returning from experimental medical treatments in France, collapses in public, AIDS becomes a national issue.

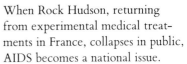

MADD: Mothers Against Drunk Driving

1
9
8
5

RENOVATIONS

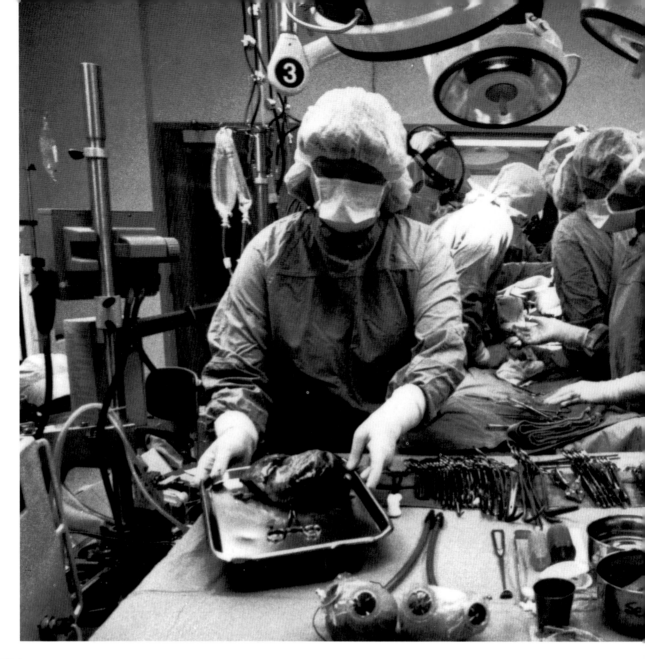

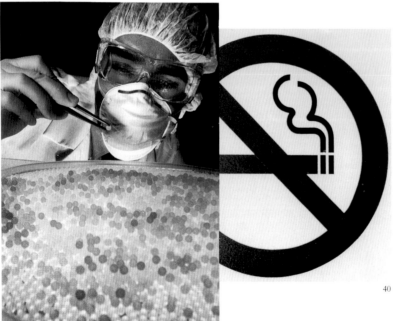

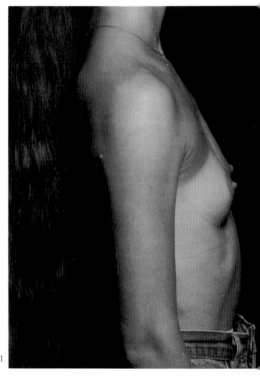

39

40

41

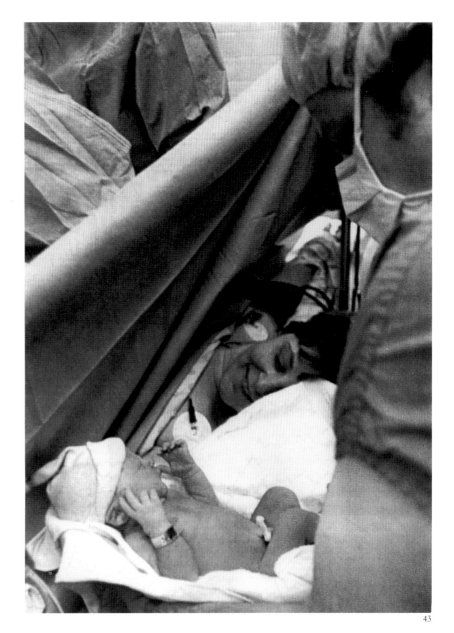

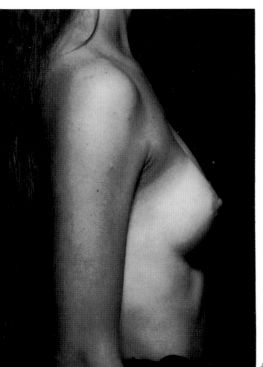

Clockwise from lower
left: Testing blood for
the AIDS virus; heart
transplant; *in vitro* baby;
Brazil; silicone; popular
American Institute of
Graphic Art image

38

43

42

44

45

DIVERSIONS

"Just Say No": Vice President George Bush, in the vanguard of the war on drugs, with an intercepted cocaine delivery. Soon the Senate's Foreign Relations Subcommittee on Narcotics would discover that the contra supply network was being supported in part by drug trafficking and that U.S. agencies knew it.

46

"Where's the beef?"

From top, left to right: Shakespeare in Seattle (Ashland's fiftieth); a new food called Tofutti; "English Country Houses" at the National Gallery; Kurosawa's *Ran*; Vanna White: "Wheel of Fortune"; Claus von Bulow; *Shoah*; Englund's "Freddy": *A Nightmare on Elm Street*; *Titanic* china; crystal channeling; creative hair statement

58

59

In New York (top), the "welcome home" parade for Vietnam vets. Above, Vietnamese immigrants fish the coastal waters off New Orleans.

"I don't resent his popularity. Good Lord, I co-starred with Errol Flynn once." —Reagan on Gorbachev

"I'm the ogre at the moment for Whites." —South African Bishop Desmond Tutu, winner of the 1984 Nobel
Peace Prize

JAMES BEARD, b. 1903
Chef

YUL BRYNNER, b. 1920
Actor

RUTH GORDON, b. 1896
Actress

ROBERT GRAVES, b. 1895
Writer

ROCK HUDSON, b. 1925
Actor

LEON KLINGHOFFER, b. 1916
Victim of terrorism

HENRY CABOT LODGE, b. 1902
Diplomat

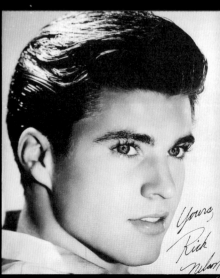

RICK NELSON, b. 1940
Singer

EUGENE ORMANDY, b. 1899
Conductor

70

MICHAEL REDGRAVE, b. 1908 71
Actor

SIMONE SIGNORET, b. 1921 72
Actress and writer

POTTER STEWART, b. 1915 73
Supreme Court justice

AIDS death toll: 12,097

ORSON WELLES, b. 1915 74
Actor and director

E. B. WHITE, b. 1899 75
Writer

1986

·Who's Kiddin' Who?·

SAM FULLER   1

...OLIVER STONE   2

GEORGE JEAN NATHAN   3

...FRANK RICH   4

1929-1968

"...*Speed up the day when all God's children, black man and white man, Jews and Gentiles, Protestants and Catholics, will be able to join hands and sing the words of the old Negro spiritual: 'Free at last! Free at last! Thank God Almighty, we are free at last!'*"

—MARTIN LUTHER KING, JR.

January 28: Ellison Onizuka, Mike Smith, Christa McAuliffe, Dick Scobee, Greg Jarvis, Ron McNair, and Judy Resnick perish in the space shuttle *Challenger* disaster.

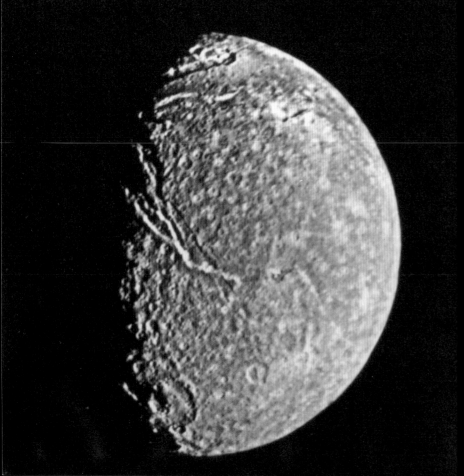

Voyager II photograph of Titania, one of Uranus's fifteen moons.

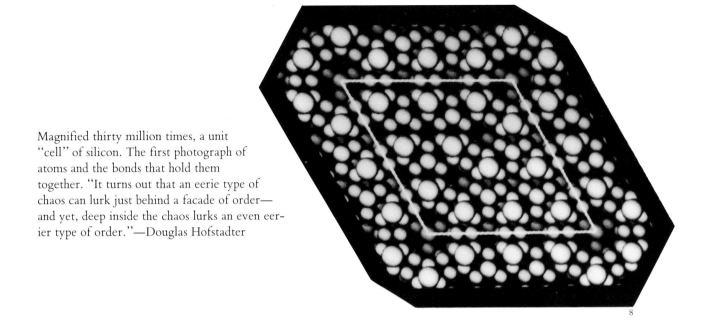

Magnified thirty million times, a unit "cell" of silicon. The first photograph of atoms and the bonds that hold them together. "It turns out that an eerie type of chaos can lurk just behind a facade of order— and yet, deep inside the chaos lurks an even eerier type of order."—Douglas Hofstadter

8

1
9
8
6

9

Rwanda National Park: A local boy becomes involved in the fate of the mountain gorilla.

10

Techies: A hubbub of PCs swarms east from Silicon Valley.

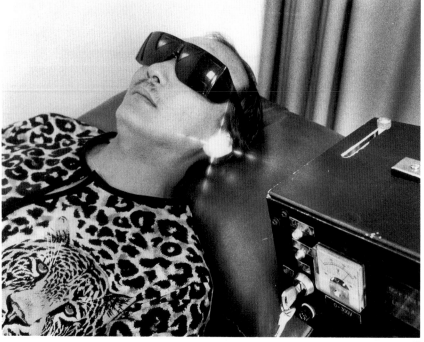

11

Left, laser-beam acupuncture.

1
9
8
6

14

15

16

17

A refurbished *Liberty Enlightening the World* at her centennial celebration

18

*"We will not forget that Liberty
has here made her home,
nor shall her chosen altar be neglected."*
—PRESIDENT GROVER CLEVELAND,
at the 1886 unveiling

20

19

21

22

23

Underground Railroad: Three hundred congregations, a Methodist
seminary, eleven universities, nineteen cities, and the entire state of New
Mexico got involved in the Sanctuary movement. The government
prosecuted founders Rev. John Fife, Jim Corbett, and four others for
harboring illegal aliens and barred any testimony pertaining to
humanitarian or religious motives.

El Salvador: "Mothers who dance for the dead"

Popular uprising ousts Ferdinand Marcos in the Philippines. Wife Imelda smuggles out shoes.

25

26

Artist and social activist Keith Haring gives away signed posters in New York's Central Park.

"Homosexual behavior is not a fundamental right," wrote Justice Byron White in the U.S. Supreme Court's majority opinion upholding Georgia's sodomy law. "Only the most willful blindness," wrote Justice Harry Blackmun in his dissent, could obscure "the connection between sexuality and the right to privacy."

"We should abandon the concept of sodomy," wrote heterosexual columnist Roy Blount, Jr., "...and give [it] a new civic name: denversion, miamy, minneapolism..."

1
9
8
6

28

29

30

31

Gray Panthers

A craze for Cabbage Patch dolls

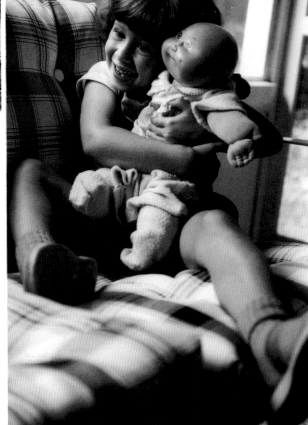

1
9
8
6

Outnumbered by cats

37

DIVERSIONS

Magic (left); New York Mets win the World Series (below). Opposite, left to right from top: Weaver: *Aliens*; "Golden Girls"; *WWD*; skateboards; Shepherd, Willis: "Moonlighting"; California cuisine; return of classic Coke; Emily Dickinson (1830–1886); Martin: *Little Shop of Horrors*; Bobby Ewing resurrected; Hurt (*Kiss of the Spider Woman*), Huston (*Prizzi's Honor*), and Page (*A Trip to Bountiful*); Oprah

38

FASHION VICTIMS 19

Coca-Cola
Trade-mark®
CLASSIC
ORIGINAL

1987

· Who's Kiddin' Who? ·

ALFRED HITCHCOCK

...STEVEN SPIELBERG

WILLIAM SHAWN

...ROBERT GOTTLIEB

Opposite, above: Pulaski, Tennessee, birthplace of the
Ku Klux Klan. Below, Jean Griffith awaits
the verdict in the trial for the Howard Beach
slaying of her son Michael.

Holocaust memorial (far left) defaced in Skokie, Illinois; Klaus Barbie (left), the "Butcher of Lyon," goes on trial; (below) Israeli soldiers and Palestinian refugees, the Gaza Strip

8

9

10

New Yorkers, tired of crime and intimidation by street punks, were polarized by the case of Bernhard Goetz (above), who shot four young black men in the subway—two in the back. Goetz was acquitted of manslaughter charges.

Day of Outrage: "Everybody remembers the first time they were taught that part of the human race was Other. That's a trauma. It's as if I told you your left hand was not part of your body." —Toni Morrison

When the Senate opened its investigation of Iran-contra, most of the major players testified. In the loop: Hashemi Rafsanjani, Manuel Noriega, John Poindexter, Bud McFarlane, and Oliver North, who said he still thought "it was a neat idea."

19

20

21

18

22

23

In El Salvador, an antigovernment protest

24

25

26

27

28

Some were saved, some were not. Opposite: A family shelter in St. Louis, Missouri (top), and a day care center (below). This page, from top: Jessica McClure, trapped in an abandoned well in Midland, Texas, for fifty-eight hours; Lisa Steinberg; Baby M.

Swaggart (right), caught with prostitute: "I have sinned."

30

Tammy Faye and Jim Bakker (below). "[The ministers] represented God, and I loved God so much." —Jessica Hahn

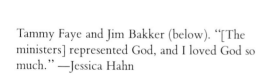

31

"God could call Oral Roberts home in March....I'm asking you to help extend my life." —Oral Roberts (above). He asked each follower to send $100.

32

The Electronic Church

"The old sawdust trail, sort of upgraded."
—Jimmy Swaggart

33

34

35

36

Pope John Paul II's first visit, as pontiff, to his homeland. His world tour eventually brought him to San Francisco and a confrontation with "The Sisters of Perpetual Indulgence," early supporters of condom use.

Hemophiliac Jason Robertson, age seven, was barred from school in Illinois. His mother successfully fought for a separate classroom for HIV-positive children.

The Names Project

Activists bring a quilt of 1,800 panels commemorating those dead from AIDS to Washington, D.C. This year President Reagan makes his first public statement about the disease.

A flag commemorates the day ten years before that Puerto Rican nationalists took over the Statue of Liberty. Below, a year after it upheld Georgia's sodomy law, activists demonstrate in front of the U.S. Supreme Court.

Opposite: Though Baby Doc fled, Haiti's free elections were attended by Ton Ton Macoutes. Below right, Sri Lankans fleeing their civil war are guided to safety by a U.S. military helicopter.

41

42

43

45

46

October 12: "Let me not be alone in the back of the crowd as I tip my hat to my longtime colleagues on the economic barricades. Thank you, Mr. Gilder, Mr. Kemp, Mr. Laffer, Mr. Mundell, Mr. Roberts, Mr. Ture, Mr. Wanneski, and all the others who helped create the economic miracle."
—Richard W. Rahn, Chief Economist, U.S. Chamber of Commerce, in the *Wall Street Journal*

October 19

48   49   50

Three Divas: Hildegard Behrens (left), Teresa Stratas, Annie Lennox

· *Who's Kiddin' Who?* ·

51   52

Two Rings: Maestro Pierre Boulez (left) conducted the 1976 Bayreauth Centennial Ring, first broadcast in the United States in 1983...Maestro James Levine conducting his new Ring Cycle at the Met

53

Three Raisins

DIVERSIONS

From top, left to right: Shroud of Turin examined; Sistine Chapel restored; Dr. Ruth; David Mamet; Nancy costars with Raisa; Dwight Gooden; "L.A. Law"; Bertolucci's *The Last Emperor*; Wilby, Grant: *Maurice*; Judge Bork rejected; Spuds McKenzie

Vogueing

67

Break dancing

68

Lesser short-nosed fruit bats: (1) They eat bugs, and (2) without them, we would have no baobab trees or organ-pipe cacti.

Left, antitreaty protesters declare that Chippewa fishermen (below, with spear) will empty northern Wisconsin lakes of fish.

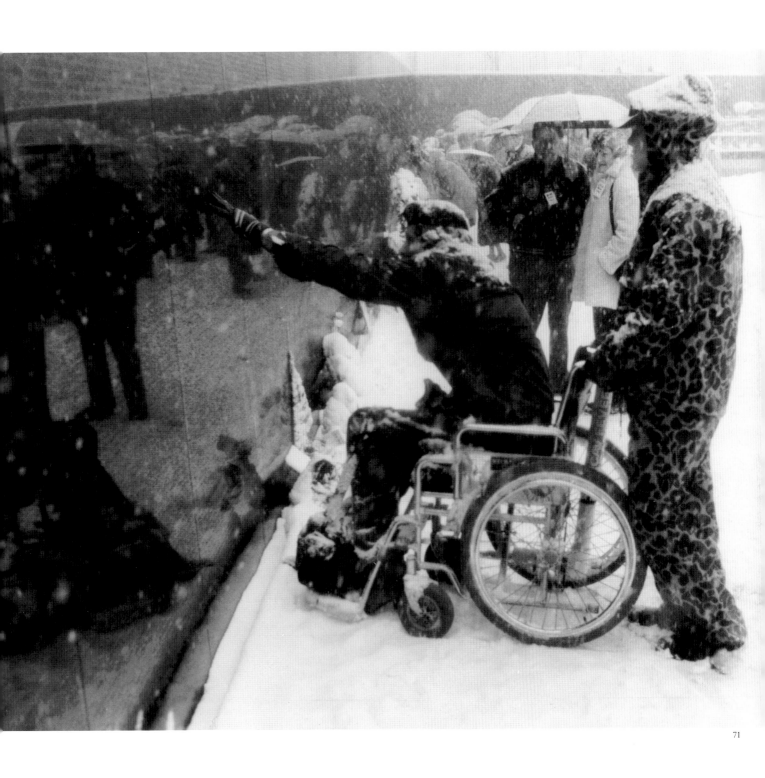

MARY ASTOR, b. 1906 [72]
Actress and writer

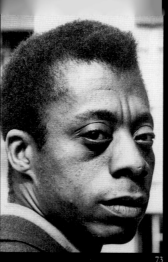

JAMES BALDWIN
b. 1924 [73]
Writer

RAY BOLGER, b. 1904 [74]
Actor

WILLIAM CASEY
b. 1913 [75]
CIA chief

BOB FOSSE, b. 1927 [76]
Choreographer

JACKIE GLEASON, b. 1916 [77]
Actor

RITA HAYWORTH, b. 1918 [78]
Actress
FRED ASTAIRE, b. 1899
Dancer

JASCHA HEIFITZ, b. 1901 [79]
Musician

RUDOLF HESS, b. 1894 [80]
Hitler's deputy

JOHN HUSTON, b. 1906 [8]
Film director

AIDS death toll: 38,858

PRIMO LEVI, b. 1919

Writer

82

LIBERACE, b. 1919

Entertainer

83

CHARLES LUDLUM, b. 1943

Actor and writer

8

GERALDINE PAGE, b. 1924

Actress

85

JACQUELINE DU PRÉ, b. 1945

Musician

86

ANDRÉS SEGOVIA, b. 1894

Musician

87

DOUGLAS SIRK, b. 1900

88

ANDY WARHOL, b. 1928

89

HAROLD WASHINGTON, b. 1922

90

1988

· *Who's Kiddin' Who?* ·

HARRY TRUMAN

...DAN QUAYLE

LUCY AND RICKY

...DAN AND ROSEANNE

5

Inner-city growth industry: A consolidated drug market brought out a new drug called "crack," making the yuppie drug of choice one everybody could afford.

6

Cabrini Green, Chicago's massive vertical ghetto. Residents dubbed it "High Rise Hell."

7

Take back the neighborhood: Brooklyn residents point out crack dens.

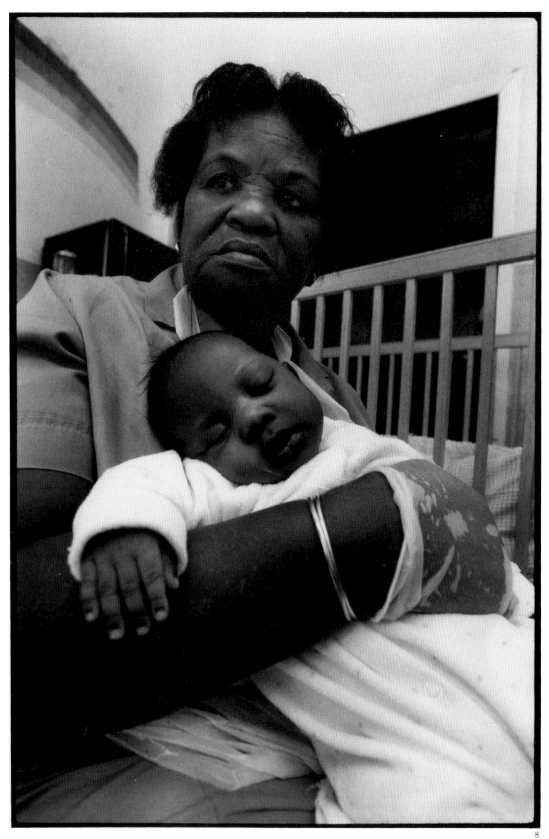

8

Hale House, Harlem: Social worker holds a child born addicted.

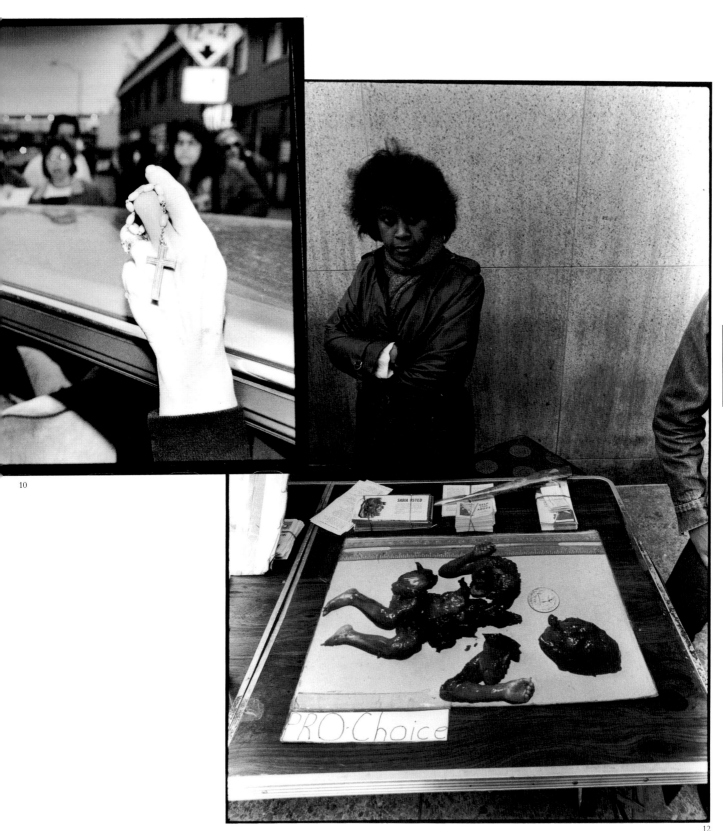

10

12

Christian fundamentalist shows photo of alleged aborted
fetus on Forty-second Street, New York.

Pro-choice escorts at clinics in
Fort Wayne, Indiana, and
Atlanta, Georgia

Convention '88: At top, Rosa Parks with Jesse Jackson. His supporters said, "We offered you Moses..." Above, Michael Dukakis, card-carrying member of the ACLU. "It used to be enough to brand a critic as a radical or a leftist to make people turn away. Now we need only to call him a liberal. Soon 'moderate' will be the m-word." —E. L. Doctorow

Mainstreet USA Welcomes VICE PRESIDENT GEORGE BUSH

ST. CHARLES, MISSOURI

PAID FOR BY BUSH, QUAYLE '88

16

"There is a story about a fellow named Willie Horton who, for all I know, may end up being Dukakis's running mate." —Lee Atwater, George Bush's campaign manager. "Watch my Vice Presidential decision. That will tell all." —George Bush

Neil Bush, son of the President and former board member of the failed Silverado S&L

17

19

20

The RJR-Nabisco takeover was the largest leveraged buyout in Wall Street history. At top, George Roberts and Henry Kravis sign the papers. The cake was eaten at the celebratory dinner. The layoffs followed....

18

Closed bank

...closed beach

24   Ozone hole

25

Clockwise from top left: Woburn,
Massachusetts: Jessica Aufiero, one of
two survivors of twelve leukemia
cases related to water contamination;
Brazil: an area the size of Kansas
falls; chieftains from seventy-six
tribes dance in defense of the
Yaṇomani.

26

27

Lockerbie, Scotland: Pan Am flight 103

204

28

29

Belfast, Northern Ireland

·Who's Kiddin' Who?·

Donna Karan for lots of folks

...Christian Lacroix for some folks

COUTURE

Gianni Versace

Giorgio Armani

Tom Wolfe dubbed the Ralph Lauren flagship store "Saville Pseud."

40

Some folks: Trump, Moschbacher, Steinberg

Yves Saint Laurent

43

Gianfranco Ferre's evening wear

Emanuel Ungaro's wedding gown

HIGH FASHION

DIVERSIONS

Opposite, top, left to right: Bono of U-2 with Grammy; Eugene O'Neill (1888–1953); Gish, Davis: *Whales of August*. Below, hip-hop: Grand Master Flash; Run-DMC; Doug E. Fresh; Stetsonic and friends

49

50

51

1
9
8
8

52

WE LOVE PEACE! WE MARCH FOR A PEACEFUL WORLD

核兵器のない平和な世界

SSDⅢの成功に向けての市民準備会　THE RREPARATORY COMMITTEE TOWAR

53

The United States
makes reparations to
Japanese-Americans
interned during World
War II.

The Iran-Iraq war ends
with a U.N. resolution.
Iraqi soldiers celebrate.

54

DIVINE (GLENN MILSTEAD)
b. 1946

Actor

JOHN HOUSEMAN, b. 1902

Producer and actor

ROBERT JOFFREY, b. 1930

Choreographer

FRANCISCO MENDES, b. 1944

Rain forest activist

LOUISE NEVELSON, b. 1899

Sculptor

ISAMU NOGUCHI, b. 1904

Sculptor and set designer

LOIS WILSON, b. 1891

Cofounder, Al-Anon Family Group

AIDS death toll: 58,360

IN REMEMBRANCE OF ALL VICTIMS
OF LOCKERBIE AIR DISASTER
WHO DIED ON 21st DECEMBER 1988

1989

· Who's Kiddin' Who? ·

GARY COOPER   1

...KEVIN COSTNER   2

MARILYN MONROE   3

...MADONNA   4

5

"Read My Lips": Bush and his chief campaign strategist. Before his death from cancer, Lee Atwater apologized for the Willie Horton campaign.

St. Paul, Virginia: Mineworkers win their benefits back from Pittstown Coal.

6

Venice, California: "Sarge," with skaters

7

Robert Mapplethorpe in Cleveland. "... A requirement that literature or
art conform to some norm prescribed by an official smacks of an ideology
foreign to our system." —Justice William O. Douglas, 1946

New York City: Residence and garden of the Mayor of Tompkins Square Park

10

Native American dancing in Queens

Restoration of Ellis Island

11

Philadelphia, Mississippi: Retracing the route of the Freedom Riders on their twenty-fifth anniversary. Montgomery, Alabama (below): Civil Rights Memorial, designed by Maya Ying Lin, at the Southern Poverty Law Center.

*"In wilderness
lies the preservation
of the world."*
—HENRY DAVID THOREAU

Recycling

Sugar Bear Tract, Washington:
Environmentalist confronts logger
in old-growth forest.

14

15

16

Earth Day

17

"The theory or fancy that Eden was in the Persian Gulf casts an odd meaning on the region's oil. . . . All that Arab oil may be the residue of Eden. . . . When I hit the gas, I'm a burner of Eden."

—MICHAEL VENTURA

1
9
8
9

Prince William Sound, Alaska: Exxon *Valdez* oil spill

San Francisco, October 18: Earthquake

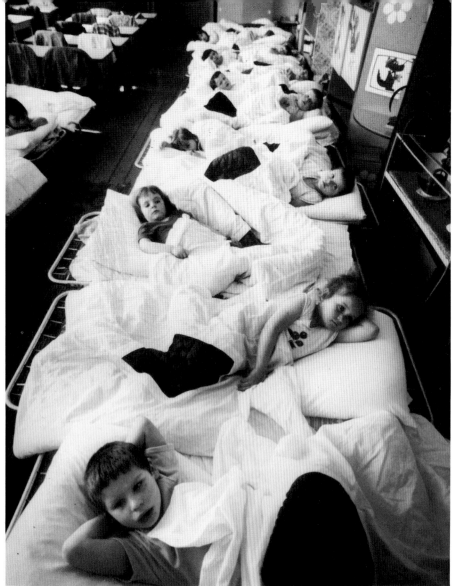

Children's ward, Chernobyl;
AIDS ward (below), Romania

20

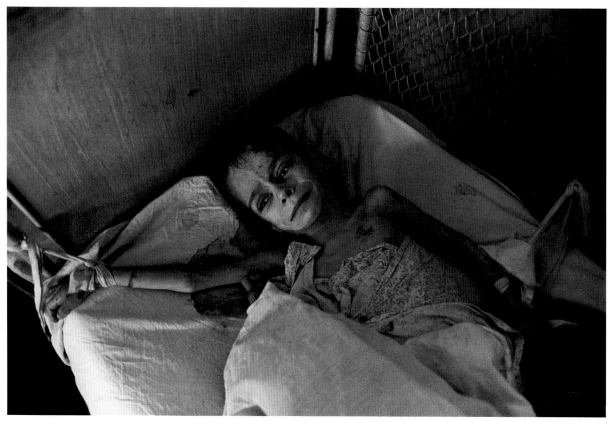

21

22

Elections bring the Salvadoran right wing into power. "After nine years of war, there is a nostalgia for the better, more secure life under the *padróne*. There is another matter: in the hamlets, there is the widely held suspicion that authorities know who you voted for." —Robert White, former U.S. ambassador to El Salvador. Above, the rector of Catholic University, five other priests, their cook, and her daughter are killed by the National Guard.

23

24

Beijing: 150,000 students chant "Down with dictatorship!
Long live freedom!"

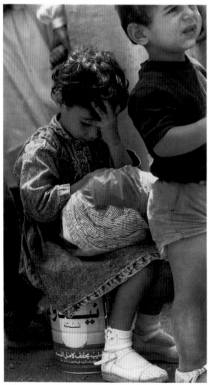

Yahoun, Lebanon: Small
refugee from Beirut rests
on a can of powdered
milk.

Tehran: Mourners mob Khomeini's bier.

Panama: Noriega's "centurions" confront voters three days after he stole the election from Guillermo Endarra (right). Endarra was beaten with a pipe minutes later. "Something has to give," said one State Department official, "but I don't know what."

Berlin Wall, 1961–1989

General Wojciech Jaruzelski and Lech Walesa at the first session of the new Polish Senate.

Romania: Nicolae Ceauşescu is overthrown.

1
9
8
9

"An old wise man said, 'If there once was light why should there be darkness again?'" —Alexander Dubcek, here with Václav Havel, Czechoslovakia

Russian soldiers, Moscow

34

American soldier, Panama. One A.M., December 20: General
Manuel Noriega waits until he hears actual gunfire and rockets
before pulling on his pants and departing La Siesta, a "recre-
ation club." It takes the U.S. Army four days to track him
down.

ALVIN AILEY, b. 1931 [53]

Choreographer

FRAN ALLISON, b. 1908 [54]

TV den mother

LUCILLE BALL, b. 1911 [55]

Actress

**SAMUEL BECKETT
b. 1906** [56]

Writer

IRVING BERLIN, b. 1888 [57]

Composer

SALVADOR DALI, b. 1904 [58]

Artist

BETTE DAVIS, b. 1904 [5]

Actress

BARTLETT GIAMATTI [60]

HIROHITO, b. 1901 [61]

ABBIE HOFFMAN, b. 1936 [62]

VLADIMIR HOROWITZ [63]

BILLY MARTIN, b. 1928 [64]
Baseball manager

LAURENCE OLIVIER [65]
b. 1907
Actor

CLAUDE PEPPER, b. 1900 [66]
Activist and politician

GILDA RADNER, b. 1946 [67]
Actress

ANDREI SAKHAROV [68]
b. 1921
Activist and scientist

I. F. STONE, b. 1907 [69]
Journalist

[70]

Red Square, Moscow: Toppled
statue of Feliks E. Dzerzhinski,
founder of CHEKA, the notorious
Soviet secret police

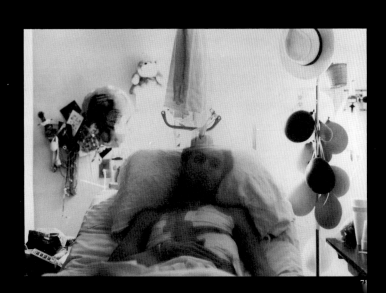

[71]

Terrorists to Reason

ELLIOTT ABRAMS
Assistant Secretary of State for Latin American Affairs

PAT BUCHANAN
White House Communications Director

GEN. CARLOS EUGENIO VIDES CASANOVA
Commander, El Salvador National Guard

GEN. SAMUEL K. DOE
President of Liberia

DAVID DUKE
Former KKK Grand Wizard

DR. ROBERT GALLO
AIDS researcher

ROBERT GATES
CIA Director

ANN BURFORD GORSUCH
EPA administrator

JEANE J. KIRKPATRICK
U.S. Ambassador to the U.N.

ARTHUR LAFFER
Financial consultant

RITA LAVELLE
Director, EPA Hazardous Waste Program

MENGISTU HAILE MARIAM
President of Ethiopia

MOBUTO SESE SEKO
President of Zaire

13

JOHN CARDINAL O'CONNOR
Archbishop of New York

14

SAMUEL PIERCE
Housing (HUD) Secretary

15

GEN. AUGUSTO PINOCHET
President of Chile

16

POL POT
Supreme Khmer Rouge Leader

17

FERDINAND ST. GERMAIN
*Chairman, House Banking
Committee*

18

JOHN SHAD
*Chairman, Securities and
Exchange Commission*

19

JOHN SUNUNU
*Bush White House
Chief of Staff*

20

EDWARD TELLER
Physicist and defense strategist

21

RANDALL TERRY
Operation Rescue founder

22

MARGARET THATCHER
Prime Minister of Great Britain

23

KURT WALDHEIM
President of Austria

24

VERNON WALTERS
Special Envoy to President Reagan

25

MOHAMMED ZIA UL-HAQ
President of Pakistan

26

235

HEARTS OF THE EIGHTIES

From top, left to right: Mother Hale (Hale House); Jimmy and Rosalynn Carter (Habitat for Humanity); the Dalai Lama; Mitch Snyder (Coalition for the Homeless); David Lange (Prime Minister, New Zealand); Vanessa Redgrave (activist); John Fife (Sanctuary); Dr. Robert Coles (child psychiatrist); Jim Hightower (politician); Jim Henson (Muppetmaster); Sam Donaldson (reporter); Sting (activist); C. Everett Koop (Surgeon General); Alice Miller (writer)

STILL GOING STRONG AT DECADE'S END

From top, left to right: Carlo Maria Giulini (conductor); Angela Lansbury (actress); Sir John Gielgud (actor); Mother Teresa; William Kunstler (lawyer); Gore Vidal (writer); Henry B. Gonzalez (politician); Dr. Seuss (writer); *The Wizard of Oz* at fifty; Leonard Bernstein (composer); Alvin Ailey's dance company; Julie Harris (actress); anti-American protester in Jordan

PICTURE CREDITS AND NOTES

Abbreviations:
G = Gamma-Liaison
I = Impact Visuals
L = Lester Glassner Collection
M = Magnum
N = New York Times Pictures
P = Photo Researchers
U = UPI/Bettmann Newsphotos
W = Wide World Photos
WWD = Women's Wear Daily

All uncredited photographs are from the collection of the author.

Endpapers: NASA.

FIRST FAMILIES
"…we love television because television brings us a world in which television does not exist." —Barbara Ehrenreich, *The Worst Years of Our Lives*. **1** White House. The second Mrs. Reagan with her family. **2** W. The first Mrs. Reagan with her family at Falcon Crest. **3** W. The Ewings at South Fork. **4** U. Millie Bush *en famille*. **5** W. The Huxtables at home in Brooklyn. **6** W. Alf and his charges.

1980
1, 2 L. **5, 6** W. Total 444 hostages taken November 4, 1979, returned home January 20, 1991. **7** M: Abbas. "I beg God to cut off the hands of all evil foreigners and all their helpers." —The Ayatollah Khomeini. The U.S. declared Iran a "terrorist nation" and imposed an arms embargo. **8, 9** W. Fifty-two Americans were seized by Iranian militants at the Teheran embassy. **10, 11** U. **12** W.

Only 28% of U.S. homes had an "Ozzie & Harriet" setup; 80% of working women earned 64¢ to a man's dollar. The ERA was approved by Congress in 1972; by 1977 it was ratified by 35 states, and had five years to win the three additional needed for full ratification. **13** Michael Soluri. Steinem quoted by Jimmy Breslin, *Newsday*, 2/13/92. **14** Marilyn Nance. **15** M: Richard Kalvar. West Point Class of 1980: 62 female cadets. 4/11/80: U.S. Equal Opportunities Commission made sexual harassment of women in the workplace illegal; Phyllis Schlafly, leader of the anti-ERA forces, before the Senate investigating committee: "Sexual harassment on the job is not a problem for virtuous women, except in the rarest of cases." **16** U. Farm incomes had dropped 75% since 1967. **17** W. Detroit: Chrysler posted $536.1 million loss; Ford posted $595 million loss; GM posted $567 million loss. "…nothing symbolized the industrial decline of the United States more than its automobile industry." —Haynes Johnson,

Sleepwalking Through History. **18** U. **19** G: Etienne Montes. **20, 22** M: Susan Meiselas. **21, 23** M: Eli Reed. Between 1980 and 1987, 40,000 Salvadorans were killed by government death squads in the civil war that began 10/79 between the U.S.-backed junta and the FMLN rebels. After D'Aubuisson was denied a U.S. visa on grounds of terrorist activity, Jesse Helms had the restriction lifted; this was seen as "a sign that the new administration would tolerate the activity of the far right, however violent" (Clifford Krauss, *Inside Central America*). **24, 25** W. **26** L. "Miami Vice": Don Johnson and Philip Michael Thomas. **27** U. **28, 29** W. "If you're white, you're right. / If you're brown, hang around. / If you're black, get back."—street doggerel; 18 were killed in the three-day Miami riots. **30** M: Richard Kalvar. **31** W. **32** M: Rene Burri. Before his nomination for Reagan's vice president, George Bush publicly "opposed Republican proposals for cutting tax rates unless such reductions were accompanied by spending cuts. He supported the Equal Rights Amendment and a woman's right to choose abortion...[and] told a TV reporter that he 'regretted' having opposed the 1964 Civil Rights Act" (Jefferson Morley, *The New York Review*, 1/16/92). **33** M: Alex Webb. **35** U. **36** W. **37** G: Apesteguy-Bulka. **38** W. The CIA declared Iran-Iraq's war would last three weeks; in 1989 it reported the U.S.S.R.'s industrial strength greater than Japan's. "Were citizens deliberately deceived or were the CIA spies so befogged by their own ideological biases that they missed the reality themselves?"—William Grieder, *Who Will Tell the People?* **39** M: Sabba. Equipment failures in the desert contributed to the deaths of eight soldiers during Operation Eagle Claw. Carter's reelection still seemed possible if the hostages were freed, and the notion of an "October surprise" spawned rumors of a Republican countermove to delay release until after election day in November. **40** U. Donald T. Regan, White House Chief of Staff, 1985–1987, *For the Record*. "Collaboration is not what the public wants from the news media."—Grieder, *Who Will Tell the People?* **41, 42** W. **43, 45** CKK Advertising. Klein made the ad campaign an event itself, and "designer culture" was born. His jeans sales went from $65 million in 1979 to $110 million in 1980 (Stuart Ewan, *All Consuming Images*). **44** P: Arthur Glauborman. **46** U. **47** W. **48** John Barr. **49** NASA. "There are thousands of ringlets encircling Saturn, dense particles orbiting individually around the equator...that vary in size from dust to boulders."—NASA brochure. **50** Trix Rosen. **51** M: Leonard Freed. **52, 53** M: Susan Meiselas. Jeane Kirkpatrick, Reagan's ambassador to the U.N., responded publicly: "The nuns were not just nuns. They were political activists." **54** M: Jean Gaumy. **55** U. **56** W. Love Canal near Niagara Falls was totally evacuated after residents, led by Lois Gibbs, convinced state and federal governments that the waste in the Hooker Chemical Company's dumpsite was causing chromosomal damage. DIVERSIONS: **57** W. **58** Bettye Lane. **59** Chris Felver. **60, 66, 68** W. It wasn't until the new season that 300 million viewers in 57 countries discovered Kristin, the mistress, sister of the wife, shot J.R. **69** W. Retiring at age 52, Howe held records for most games played (1,687), most goals (801), most assists (1,049), and most points (1,850). **70** W. **71** U. OBITS: **72, 73, 74, 76, 78, 79, 80, 81, 82, 84** W. **75, 83, 85** L. **77** U.

1981

1 U. The Department of the Interior was established in 1902 under President Theodore Roosevelt's administration; it has since preserved nearly 150 million acres of land. **2.** U. James G. Watt, Reagan's secretary of the interior (1981–1983), announced budget cuts for the Environmental Protection Agency, even though the General Accounting Office had found 378,000 dangerous toxic sites and the EPA had 850 on its priority list; in 1982, the EPA reversed its stand and permitted drums of toxic waste to be buried in landfills in spite of Love Canal. **3, 5** U. Though Reagan reiterated that "Government is not the solution to our problems; government is the problem," under his administration the number of government employees rose by 150,000, government spending rose 25%, the national debt rose from 26.6% of the GNP to 43%. The inauguration cost $16.3 million, five times Carter's tab. **6** W. The hostages were freed on Inauguration Day, fueling the "October surprise" rumors. **7** M: Eugene Richards. **8** G: Etienne Montes. **9, 10, 11, 12** W: Joan Quigley. Nancy Reagan's astrologer commented: "The president should have stayed home. I could see from my charts that this was going to be a dangerous day for him." "Please," said the wounded Reagan to the surgeons about to operate, "tell me you're Republicans!" **13** W. **14** G: Makram Karim. **15** G: J. C. Francolon. Reagan's rebound "from a bullet wound lodged an inch from his heart was taken as an augury of a national turn for the better." —Johnson, *Sleepwalking Through History*. **16** U. The "dense pack," nicknamed "dunce pack," produced 50 missiles at a cost of $15 billion. **17** G: Claude Salhani. **18, 19** U. **20** W. Headmistress Jean Harris shot Dr. Herman Tarnover of *Complete Scarsdale Medical Diet* fame in 1980; she was sentenced to 15 years in 1981. **21** W. DIVERSIONS: **26** Jarry Lang. **27, 30** L. **33** U. **34** P: Nancy Pierce. **35** Al Santana. In 1969, women comprised 9% of first-year medical students; in 1987, 37%.—"Are Women Better Doctors?" *New York Times Magazine*, 4/10/88. **36** M: David Hurn. **37** Marilyn Nance. "In our fantasies, at least, we [feminists] did not want to enslave men, as *Playboy* writers liked to think, but to share the adventure." —Ehrenreich, *The Worst Years of Our Lives*. **38** M: Richard Kalvar. **39** M: Eve Arnold. **40** M: Raymond Depardon. Roberta Grandeis Gratz, *The Living City*. **41, 42, 45, 46, 47** U. **43, 44, 48, 49** W. **50** M: David Hurn. **51, 52** W. "There is no money. This is a worst-case scenario." —Dr. Walter Dowdle, GRID budget director, Centers for Disease Control. **53** G. "You can't take on tanks with running shoes." —Lech Walesa. **54** P: Ruth Perron. PATCO, one of the few unions to support Reagan, lost its certification and went bankrupt after the President replaced its members in airport towers with men and women from the armed forces. **55** G/*Fort Lauderdale News*. **56** W. OBITS: **57, 58, 60, 61, 62, 64, 65, 66** W. KKK members out looking for a black person lynched Donald. His mother, Beulah Mae Donald, and the Southern Poverty Law Center's Morris Dees sued the Klan as provocateurs and won a $7 million judgment.

1982

1, 2 W. Stanwyck never won an Oscar and had to make do with an honorary one. **3, 4** W. **5** Bart Bartholomew. **6** Bettye Lane. **7** W. "I never had any thought when I set up the CIA that it would be injected into peacetime cloak and dagger operations." —President Harry Truman, 1963. **8, 9** M: Susan Meiselas. President Duarte won 42% of the popular vote, and $129 million in U.S. aid; there were 250 political murders a week, including two U.S. land-reform agents, Michael Hammon and Marc Perlman, by the National Guard. **10** W. **11** Jarry Lang. According to NASA, the U.S. latitude's ozone layer is disappearing at twice the calculated rate. **12, 13** U. Louise B. Young, *Sowing the Wind*. **14, 15, 16, 17** Steve Rubin. **18** U. **19** Trix Rosen. **20** Anders Goldfarb. Oliver Wendell Holmes: "If there is any principle of the Constitution that more imperatively calls for attachment than any other it is the principle of free thought—not free thought for those who agree with us, but freedom for the thought that we hate." **21** U. 20% of the nation's schools attempted to ban books. On the list: *Merriam–Webster Collegiate Dictionary, The Red Badge of Courage, The Autobiography of Ben Franklin, Hamlet, Huckleberry Finn*. The U.S. government reported 23 million "functionally illiterate" adults. **22, 23** W. The Rev. Moon was sentenced to 18 months for tax fraud. **24** W. **25, 26** M: Abbas. Israel invaded to crush strongholds of the PLO and of the occupying Syrian army. **27** M: Chris Steel

Perkins. The Joint Chiefs of Staff opposed sending marines into Beirut. **28** G: Alain Mingam. Israel's defense minister, Ariel Sharon, resigned over his "grave mistake" in ignoring the possibility of revenge killings. **29** Orbis. This nonprofit teaching hospital spends 90% of its time in developing countries. **30** Curtis Compton. DIVERSIONS: **31** PBS. Mark Fowler, Reagan's new Federal Communications Commission chairman: "Television is just another appliance. It's a toaster with pictures." His deregulations eliminated public service requirements and limitations on advertising time. **34** L. AT&T broke up its "protected monopoly" and won the right to move into areas of new technology surrendered in a 1956 antitrust battle. **40** L. **35, 36, 41** W. **39** Library of Congress. **42, 43** M: Susan Meiselas. **44** M: Erich Hartmann. "…the names of the dead seem to come to life in the reflection of my own face, my own body—I know that, through this wall, they are demanding of me a response, and I don't know what to say to them.…" —Michael Ventura, *LA Weekly*, 3/29/91. OBITS: **45, 47, 48, 51, 56, 57, 59** W. **46, 55, 62** L. **49, 53, 60, 61** U. The poisoned Tylenol killed seven in Chicago and one in California.

1983

1, 2 W. **3** U. **4** W. **5** Bettye Lane. "It has now reached the point where important AIDS work cannot be undertaken because of the lack of available resources." —Edward Brandt, Assistant Secretary for Health. **6** W. Robert Dole was the undisputed leading PAC money recipient, with $3,366,305 in contributions between 1968 and 1986. The largest PAC: National Association of Realtors. **7** W. David Stockman's resignation was refused (11/81) after he admitted serious doubts about supply-side, "trickle-down," "voodoo" economics in an *Atlantic Monthly* interview; 1981 individual tax cuts of 25% and corporate tax restructuring reduced government revenues by $750 billion over five years. GE, with profits of $6.5 billion between 1981 and 1983, received an IRS rebate of $283 million. **8** U. **9** W. **10** M: Bob Adelman. **11** W. In Japanese, "Japan bashing" is *gai-atsu*. In 1982, the UAW granted $3.5 billion in "hardship contract" concessions to Ford and GM, which then gave $262 million in bonuses to their execs. **12** U. In London, Ohio, the county sheriff was forced to use signs: farmers were shouting down auctioneers. **13** NASA. Strategic Defense Initiative equals $26 billion over five years. **14** W. **15** G. **16** M: Susan Meiselas. **17** M: James Nachtway. U.S. State Department: "The Nicaraguans create a devil outside to increase internal security." A U.S. poll showed most Americans didn't know who the U.S. supported in Central America. A Salvadoran judge refused to try the military men responsible for killing the four U.S. religious and two U.S. land reform agents. **18** Bettye Lane. **19** W. Despite the bombing of the U.S. embassy in Beirut six months earlier, U.S. commanders failed "to take the security measures necessary" (Long Commission report) at marine headquarters: 241 members of the 1st Battalion, 8th Regiment died. **20** W. "Grenada…was a Soviet-Cuban colony being readied as a major military bastion to export terrorism and undermine democracy. We got there just in time." —Reagan. "…the president and his White House staff were shameless and successful using the easy victory in Grenada to wipe away the stain of the unnecessary disaster in Beirut." —Lou Cannon, *Ronald Reagan: The Role of a Lifetime*. **21** W. **22** U. DIVERSIONS: **23** Halley Erskine. **24** NASA. **25, 26, 27, 28** W. Nuclear power stations industry lost billions as plants were converted to coal, abandoned, or denied licenses. In 1989, the Energy Department announced $92 billion was needed to clean up nuclear waste. **32, 34** W. "M*A*S*H": 125 million watched the 4077th return home after 11 years and 250 episodes. **35** M: Inge Morath. **36** W. OBITS: **37, 38, 39, 40, 41, 42, 43, 44, 45, 46, 49, 50** W.

1984

1, 2, 3, 4 W. **5** NASA. **6** W. Gorbachev: "We need spiritual values. We need a revolution of the mind." **7** U. Mary Summers, Jackson's head speechwriter: "Jesse Jackson knows how to ride the waves of history better than anyone, but riding waves is a wild art…it does not require working with others to develop a plan to turn the tide." **8** M: Gilles Peress. "Yuppie" was coined to describe Hart's young urban professional supporters. **9** U. "D'Amato used HUD and in particular the New York office as his private campaign trough.…[He] has run a number of dirty political errands for Presidents Ronald Reagan and George Bush. Just last week, he voted against the attempt to override Bush's veto of the civil rights bill. That override failed by only one vote. It all looks like part of D'Amato's protection racket." —Sydney H. Schanberg, *Newsday*, 10/30/90. **10, 11** W. **12** U. Gary Wills, *The New York Review*, 1/30/92. **13** M: Eli Reed. **14** M: Gilles Peress. **15** U. Mr. Ferraro was cleared of extortion charges, 10/87. **16** M: Eli Reed. Estimated 10,000 homeless in D.C., 2 million in U.S. 49% of black children under six growing up in poverty (National Academy of Sciences). Estimated 5 million children under six living in poverty (Economic Policy Institute, D.C.). **17** U. Reagan carried 49 states. "What I want for the country above all else is that it may always be a place where a man can get rich." **18** W. For the first time in history, the Olympic games were computerized, used corporate sponsorship, and made a profit. **19, 21, 22, 23, 24, 25, 28, 29** W. **20, 26, 27** U. **30, 31** I: Catherine Smith. **32** I: Orde Eliason. Jon Qwelane, South African journalist: "We can make common cause. But the struggle in South Africa really cannot be fought nonracially. Black kids are dying. White kids are not dying" (quoted in William Finnegan, *Dateline Soweto*). "How a political system treats children reveals its true character." —Richard Falk, Professor, International Law, Princeton. Between 1984 and 1986, 300 children under 18 were killed, 1,000 wounded, 11,000 detained without trial, and 173,000 held in prisons awaiting trial. South Africans set up a new tricameral parliament with its 23 million blacks, 73% of the population, denied representation. **33** G: Pablo Bartholomew. After six accidents in six years and a company report warning of "a serious potential for sizeable release of toxic materials," Union Carbide's pesticide factory leaked gas killing 3,329, radically harming 30,000 to 40,000, and injuring 200,000. **34, 35** W. 24 abortion clinics were bombed. Justice Lewis Powell, in his majority decision (6/83) reaffirming *Roe v. Wade*: "…we held in *Roe v. Wade* that the right of privacy, grounded in the concept of personal liberty guaranteed by the Constitution, encompasses a woman's right to decide whether to terminate her pregnancy." **36** W. RICO was the successful courtroom tool used against the Mafia by the Department of Justice and FBI. "It was sort of like George Kennan's containment policy of the Soviet Union. We tried it and by God it worked." —Robert Blakey, chief architect of RICO. DIVERSIONS: **37** M: David Hurn. **38** W. Abdul-Jabbar retired 4/23/89. **39** W. Reagan, 73, was the oldest President in U.S. history. **40** Xavier Vivanco. The century's greatest operatic voices were delivered with "truer" tonality on CDs. Callas became an industry; the legendary de los Angeles (shown as Manon in 1956) celebrated 45 years of singing in 1989. **41** Luigi Cassaniga. **42, 43** W. **47, 48** L. OBITS: **49, 52, 55, 57, 58, 59, 60, 62, 64** W. **50, 61, 63** L. **53** U.S. Army. **54** U.

1985

1 U. Leontyne Price retired; at her 1961 debut, she received the longest ovation after a single aria in Met history. **2, 3, 4, 5** W. The World Court condemned U.S. contra support, calling it "the intervention of one state in the internal affairs of the other." **6** WWD. **7** U. **8** W. **9, 10** P: Spencer Grant, Bobbie Kingsley. **11, 12**

Michael Soluri. **13** U. S&Ls: In 1980, Congress removed ceilings on interest rates to depositors and increased federal insurance to cover $100,000 in deposits; in 1982, Garn–St. Germain allowed thrifts to expand investments beyond home loans while Farm Home Loan Bank Board (FHLBB) head Richard Pratt deregulated to allow single owners in lieu of 400 stockholders, and "scores of investors like Charles Keating moved in swiftly, turning the thrift industry into a huge casino where only the taxpayer could lose" (Steve V. Roberts, *U.S. News & World Report*, 1/10/90). **14, 15** I: Martha Tabor. Farm sale near York, Pennsylvania. **16** W. An estimated 1,000 pandas are all we have left. **17** W. Reagan accepted an invitation to visit, "in the spirit of reconciliation," a German military cemetery where more than 30 members of Waffen SS were buried. Though he never left the U.S. during WWII, Reagan told both Simon Wiesenthal and Israel's Prime Minister Shamir that he had personally filmed a Nazi concentration-camp liberation. "The charm of Ronald Reagan is not just that he kept telling us screwy things, it was that he believed them all. No wonder we trusted him, he never lied to us." —Molly Ivins, *Savvy*, 10/89. **18, 19** W. *Rainbow Warrior* was protesting French nuclear testing in the South Pacific; the explosion killed a Greenpeace member. The French defense minister resigned and the intelligence agency's director was dismissed. **20** M: Gerald Hilton. Pursuing MOVE, a radical political group, police firebombed 61 row houses, killing 11; a grand jury found Mayor Goode guilty of "morally reprehensible behavior" and Police Commissioner George Sambor resigned. **21** I: Donna Binder. Hate-motivated crimes: "Homosexuals are probably the most frequent victim." —National Institute of Justice. **22** U. Attacks in Rome and Vienna, aimed at Israel, left 18 killed and 110 wounded. **23** Jim Tynan. **24, 25** M: Sebastiao Salgado. Ethiopia suffered drought, deforestation, civil war, and government corruption. The U.S. sent more than $300 million to aid the 7.5 million famine victims. **26** Jim Tynan. **27** U. **28, 29, 30, 31** W. MTV was born in 1981; by 1985 it had 24.2 million viewers. **32** Federal Photos Montreal. Awareness of the alcoholic family's dynamics increased through the proliferation of 12-Step programs like AA, Al-Anon Family Group, and ACOA. "Many children of alcoholic parents survive by withdrawing into themselves and creating their own reality. They invent themselves. They learn to deny reality. Something similar seems to have happened with Reagan." —Johnson, *Sleepwalking Through History*. **33** W. MADD, formed in 1980. Its lobbying helped cut drunk-driving deaths by 30%. **34** W. **35** Mark Richards. American youth spent an average of 13 hours a week on sports or exercise and 50 hours a week on TV or video games. "The great majority know the importance of fitness. But they have not taken the action themselves. Americans are not as fit as they think they are." —Dr. Michael McGuiness, U.S. Department of Health. **36, 37** W. Liberty's torch and arm were closed in 1916. **38** U. **39** W. By 1983, blood was suspected, along with semen, to be a conduit for the HIV virus. Blood-bank testing did not begin until March 1985. **40** W. Cigarette warning label: "May I suggest: 'Use of this product results in artificial and temporary weight loss and is accompanied by the death of ¼ of its users." —Dr. Michele Block, director, Women vs. Smoking Network, letter in *The New York Times*, 3/19/91. **41, 42, 43** U. **44** L. DIVERSIONS: **45** U. Bush was head of the South Florida Task Force and National Narcotics Border Interdiction System, 1982–1988. **46** W. Dr. Holmberg, CDC: "We were able to show for the first time how an antibiotic-resistant bacterium can actually make its way from the barnyard to the dinner table." The UK limited antibiotic use in 1971; pharmaceutical lobbies and livestock breeders blocked a proposed U.S. ban in 1983. DIVERSIONS: **47** Ashland. There are 676 performances a year to 90% capacity in three theaters. **48, 51, 52, 55** W. **49** National Gallery. **56** Sharon Smith. **57** Anders Goldfarb.

58, 59, 60 U. Gorbachev: "Mr. President, you should keep in mind that we are not simpletons." **61** M: Ian Berry. OBITS: **62, 63, 65, 67, 68, 70, 73, 75** W. **66, 69** L.

1986

1, 2, 3 W. "I read George Jean Nathan every week." —Eve Harrington, *All About Eve*. **4** W. "Rich's taste is essentially safe, middle of the road and consumer-oriented." —Robert Brustein, *The New Republic*, 3/16/92. **5** I: Donna Binder. King Day became a national holiday 6/2/83. **6** NASA. Subsequent reports named Morton Thiokol Company's faulty seals and NASA mismanagement as causes of the explosion. **7** NASA. Unlike other planets, Uranus lies tipped on its side with its north and south poles alternately facing the sun during its 84-year swing around the solar system; there are 16 half-ice moons like Titania. **8** IBM. **9** M: Michael Nichols. Rwanda's gorillas became a prime tourist attraction, neatly combining conservation with economics. **10, 11, 13** U. **12** P: Paul Sequeira. **15** W. **14, 16** Katherine Andriotis. Millions across America formed a human chain to raise money for the homeless. **17, 18, 21, 22** W. **19, 20** U. 6 million people, 20,000 boats, and 26 tallships from 18 countries attended Miss Liberty's birthday party. **23** I: David Vita. **24** Jim Tynan. "On July 29, 1986, Bush [head of the U.S. task force on terrorism] had traveled to Israel, where he met with Amiram Nir, the Israeli prime minister's deputy on counterterrorism.... Nir explained to the vice president that if the Iranians received the shipment, they would arrange the freeing of two hostages. Soon afterward, the U.S. acceded to Nir." —Sidney Blumenthal, *Pledging Allegiance*. **25** W. In 1983, Benigno Aquino was murdered returning to the Philippines from U.S. exile; two years later, the Filipino military was found innocent of conspiracy. Mrs. Corazon Aquino rejected the verdict and announced her candidacy in the upcoming elections; after wrongly claiming victory in the polls early in 1986, Marcos fled and Aquino was recognized by the U.S. **26** Marilyn Nance. Keith Haring (1958–1990) died of AIDS. In September 1985, Reagan apologized for saying racial segregation had ended in South Africa and seemed to withdraw his objections to limited sanctions; a year later, he vetoed a bill to impose sanctions, but Congress overrode his veto. Prime Minister Botha said: "Well, it's done. Now, maybe, they'll leave us alone." **27** Charles W. Springman. "Now the Supreme Court has made the closet unsafe." —Jean O'Leary. Justice Byron White's majority opinion claimed a "great resistance...to discover new fundamental rights not enumerated in the Constitution"—although Article 9 of the Constitution states that *The enumeration in the Constitution of certain rights shall not be construed to deny or disparage others retained by the people*. In his dissent, Justice Blackmun pointed out that "A necessary corollary of giving individuals freedom to choose how to conduct their lives is acceptance of the fact that different individuals will make different choices. It is precisely because the issues raised by this case touch the heart of what makes individuals what they are that we should be especially sensitive to the rights of those whose choices upset the majority." **28, 29, 31** M: Eugene Richards. **30** M: Paul Fusco. **33, 34** W. **35** P: Barbara Rios, Rona Beame. **36** U. DIVERSIONS: **37, 38, 49** U. **41** WWD. **42, 50** W. **44** John Sedlar. **45** Amherst. **47** Coca-Cola. **51** G: Piero Guerrini. The cruise ship *Achille Lauro* was hijacked 10/7/85 by four Palestinian terrorists; their escape plane was intercepted by U.S. Navy jets four days later. **52** U. **53, 54** W. *Frontline*: "High Crimes and Misdemeanors" (Show #906), 11/27/90. "The original Presidential Finding which Reagan had signed in December 1985, authorizing the covert shipment of arms to Iran, had been worded in such a way as to make the Iran initiative sound like nothing more than arms for hostages." —Oliver North, *Under Fire*. "I think the president knew what was going on, sure, clearly when he signed the finding and probably before." —William Casey, CIA chief. Yet in November 1986, Reagan said: "We did not—repeat—did not trade weapons or anything else for hostages nor will we." By the end of December, he was saying: "I was not fully informed." Finally, in March 1987, he made this odd confession: "A few months ago, I told the American people that I did not trade arms for hostages. My heart and my best intentions still tell me that is true, but the facts and the evidence tell me it is not." OBITS: **55, 61, 64, 70** U. **56, 57, 59, 65, 66, 67, 68, 69, 72, 73, 74, 75, 76, 77** W. **58, 63** L. **60** WWD.

1987

1, 2 W. Neither Hitchcock nor Spielberg ever won an Oscar; each received the Irving Thalberg Award for "life achievement," Hitch in 1968. **3, 4** *New York Times*. William Shawn edited *The New Yorker* (1952–1987) until its new owner, S. I. Newhouse, replaced him with Robert Gottlieb, publisher of Knopf, a division of Newhouse-owned Random House. **5** I: Catherine Smith. "Attitudes toward blacks that have their origin in slavery shape the nation's response to citizens of all colors, and the same attitudes have an enormous impact on the conduct of foreign policy." —William H. Grier and Price M. Cobbs, *Black Rage*. **6** I: Donna Binder. Griffith was murdered 12/20/86; three white teens were found guilty of manslaughter a year later. **7** W. Elie Wiesel: "I have an occasional nightmare now. I wake up shivering, thinking that when we die, no one will be able to persuade people that the Holocaust occurred." **8** W. Barbie, seen as a Cold War asset, was transported by the U.S. Army to Bolivia in 1953; he was arrested in 1983 and returned to France for trial. **9, 10** W. **11** W. **12** Marilyn Nance. "In 1987, the wealthiest 40% of American families received 67.8% of the national family income, the highest percent ever recorded... the poorest 40% of families received 15.4%... the lowest ever recorded." —Center on Budget and Policy Priorities. "The average gain in income of the top 1% ($134,513) was almost 6 times the income of the average family in the middle 40%." —Economic Policy Institute, Washington, D.C. In 1970, 39% of students at UCLA made "being well off financially" their top goal; in 1987, 73% (from "More College Freshmen Plan to Teach," *The New York Times*, 1/12/87). **13, 14** U. After cutting deals and wearing a wire, Boesky was sentenced to three years in prison and served one and a half; Milken went it alone and was sentenced to 10. **15** U. **16** W. The Islip (N.Y.) barge traveled 6,000 miles to six states and three countries before returning to Islip. NYC disposes of 14,329 tons of garbage daily. **17** U. Reagan said 184 times during his public testimony on Iran-contra that he could not remember events. "He sensed that we would gladly accept his loss of memory as an alibi. It had simply slipped his mind what form of government we had in our country." —Steve Tesich, *The Nation*, 1/6/92. **18, 19, 20** W. In September 1989, Poindexter claimed in court that Reagan had ordered him to lie under oath to the congressional panel. **21** W. **22** U. McFarlane received a fine and probation; Poindexter received a six-month jail sentence; North, convicted of destroying documents and obstructing Congress, was sentenced to a period of community service and fined, but this was reversed on Fifth Amendment grounds. "From North's narrow perspective, Nicaragua was not a nation with its own heritage, but a battleground where he could take revenge on international Communism for having defeated him and the men with whom he served in Vietnam." —Stephen Kinzer, *Blood of Brothers*. **23** Jim Tynan. Of the approximately 1 million Salvadorans who emigrated between 1984 and 1987, an estimated 400,000 entered the U.S. illegally. **24** M: Eli Reed. **25** P: Abraham Menashe. A Senate subcommittee began hearings on day care: 60% of mothers with children under 14 are working; 50% return to work before their child's first birthday. **26**

U. **27** Stuart Gross. Joel Steinberg, who adopted Lisa illegally, was found guilty of manslaughter 1/30/89. That same year, the Supreme Court decided that: "A state's failure to protect an individual against private violence did not deny the victim's constitutional rights." **28** W. "...one can't help conclude that it was the Sterns who were guilty of believing in magic: the idea of getting a baby for cash, bloodlessly, is a state-of-the-art yuppie fantasy." —Ehrenreich, *The Worst Years of Our Lives*. **29** Jerry Gay. **30** U. The private eye who caught Swaggart with a prostitute was hired by a former minister defrocked for adultery, a penalty engineered by Swaggart, who brought in $150 million a year and who was "silenced" for three months for his indiscretion. **31** W. **32** U. Bakker was found guilty on 24 counts of defrauding the public of $3.7 million; in 1986, he brought in $126 million but $265,000 went to hush up a sex scandal in which Hahn was a lead player. **33, 34** M: Steve McCurry. **35** W. **36** U. For the first time in history, the Vatican posted a loss: $25 million. **37** M: Paul Fusco. **38** I: Marvin Collins. "Cast your whole vote, not a scrap of paper merely, but your whole influence. A minority is powerless while it conforms to the majority; it is not even a minority then; but it is irresistible when it clogs by its whole weight." —Thoreau. **39** U. **40** I: Donna Binder. "We did not have the full degree of support from the Administration." —Dr. Mayberry, Chief Executive, Mayo Clinic, on resigning as chairman of Reagan's first AIDS committee. "Everyone detected with AIDS should be tattooed in the upper forearm, to protect common-needle users, and on the buttocks, to prevent the victimization of other homosexuals." —William F. Buckley, *New York Times*, op-ed page, 3/18/86. **41** U. **42** I: Marilyn Humphries. **43** M: Alex Webb. **44** G. **45** Jarry Lang. "If you visit Dallas or Houston or Austin or San Antonio, you can see where much of the [S&L] money wound up. It is visible in row upon row of empty office buildings and shopping centers." —Paul Zane Pilzer and Robert Deitz, *Other People's Money*. **46** Dorothy Low. **47** U. The stock market dropped 508 points, losing 22.6% of its value. "The greater irony... was that in the end what kept '87 from turning into another '29 was the very hand of the federal government that Reagan and the supply-siders had railed against." —Johnson, *Sleepwalking Through History*. "What do you call a 28-year-old trader in suspenders?" "Hey, waiter!" **49** U. **48, 50, 51, 52, 53** W. DIVERSIONS: **55.** "The monochrome that misled generations is gone forever. This is not the Sistine ceiling of the old art history books, a work of miserable individualistic prognosis and thunderous personal pessimism. This is a bright, light, colorful and uplifting Renaissance spectacle, less a warning and more of a celebration." —Waldemar Januszczak, *Sayonara, Michelangelo*. **56, 57, 58, 60, 63, 64** W. **59** U. **62** L. Vito Russo: "Slurs that would never be tolerated in reference to any other group of people are commonly used onscreen against homosexuals. Unlike racist remarks, which are almost always put in the mouth of villains and bigots, antigay comments are most frequently given to the characters with whom the audience is supposed to identify. In the last five years, fully half of the films directed at the youth market have been unconscionably homophobic." **63** W. Bork was rejected by the largest margin in Senate history. **64** W. **65, 66** Dorothy Low. Vogueing: "dancing in a style that combines the exaggerated walks and poses of runway fashion models with moves from breakdancing, hiphop, martial arts and modern dance." —Eric Pooley, *New York*, 10/15/90. **67** Luigi Cassaniga. **68** Martin D. Tuttle/Bat Conservation International, Milwaukee Public Museum. Tuttle: "Conservationists are going to have to stop dealing with just the animals that people easily relate to because they have big brown eyes or soft fur." As of this writing, there are 27 condors left in the U.S. **69, 70** I: Andrew Lichtenstein, Catherine Smith. **71** U. OBITS: **73, 74, 75, 79, 80, 82, 83, 85, 86, 87, 88, 89, 90** W. **76** U. **78, 81** L. **84** Jarry Lang.

1, 2 W. Quayle addressed the United Negro College Fund ("A mind is a terrible thing to waste") 6/89: "What a waste to lose one's mind or not to have a mind at all." **4** W. **5** Jim Tynan. "Money and drugs are the obvious immediate rewards for kids in the cocaine trade. But there is another strong motivating force, and that is the desire to show family and friends that they can succeed at something." —Terry Williams, *The Cocaine Kids*. **6, 8** M: Leonard Freed, Eugene Richards. **7** Jolie Stahl. **9** Luis Deveyra. **10** Jim Tynan. **11** U. **12** I: Kirk Condyles. In 1989, the Supreme Court upheld a Missouri ban on abortion in public hospitals; a year later, it would uphold parental notification by teens and a "gag rule" on clinicians forbidding them to discuss abortion. **13, 14** W. **15** G: Jon Simon. Ann Richards, keynote address, Democratic convention: "Poor George. He can't help it. He was born with a silver foot in his mouth." **16** W. Willie Horton, a convicted murderer, committed rape while on furlough from prison authorities; Massachusetts's furlough program was instituted by Dukakis's Republican predecessor. "It's a wonderful mix of liberalism and a big black rapist," said an anonymous member of Bush's campaign team (quoted in Blumenthal, *Pledging Allegiance*). George Bush, 5/9/88, Twin Falls, Idaho: "For 7½ years I've worked alongside him [Reagan] and I'm proud to be his partner. We've had triumphs; we've made mistakes; we've had sex . . . *setbacks*, we've had *setbacks*." **17** U. Silverado S&L lost $1 billion. "State regulators plan to close Silverado but an unnamed Washington official orders regional regulators to wait until December. The day after George Bush is elected president, Topeka-based federal regulator Kermit Mowbray signs a memo requiring Silverado's seizure." —*Time*, 10/1/90. **18, 19** Michael Fairchild. **20** Marilyn Nance. "The LBO is, after all, simply an investment technique, in which you hock the assets of a company in order to buy it—similar to a way many real estate deals are done, with second and third mortgages." —Connie Bruck, *The Predators' Ball*. In 1989, Time Inc. bought Warner Communications (WCI); they debted $11.5 billion but WCI CEO Steve Ross received the largest payout ever made to an executive in a public company: $193 million plus $1.8 million in new stock options, which could add up to hundreds of millions over his 15-year contract. Congresspeople earn $43 an hour or $89,000 yearly; a woman working full-time at minimum wage earns $3.35 an hour, or $2,000 below the poverty level, yet this year Congress rejected an increase in the minimum wage. **21** W. **22, 23** I: Kirk Condyles, Lonny Shavelson. **24** NASA. "Although with the advent of space flight it became fashionable to picture the planet as a small orb of life and light in a cold, dark vastness, that image never really sank in." —Bill McKibben, *The End of Nature*. **25** M: Michael Nichols. **26** U. **27** W. A Libyan bomb killed 11 villagers and 259 passengers. **28, 29** Jim Tynan. The IRA is partly financed by U.S. "barstool revolutionaries" in NORAID. **30, 31, 32, 33, 34, 35, 36, 37, 38, 39, 40, 41, 42, 43, 44** WWD. "Clothes are our weapons, our challenges, our visible insults. And more." —Angela Carter, *Nothing Sacred*. **45, 47** Luigi Cassaniga. **46, 52** Dorothy Low. **48** Michael Fairchild. DIVERSIONS: **49** U. **50** Library of Congress. **53** I: George Cohen. 120,000 Japanese-Americans were "relocated" to 10 internment camps. **54** W. The Iran-Iraq War was the bloodiest conflict since WWII: 1 million dead, 1.7 million wounded, and 1.5 million refugees. OBITS: **55, 56, 57, 58, 59, 60, 62** W. **61** Al-Anon Family Group.

1 L. **2** W. **3, 4** U. Fran Liebowitz: "[Madonna] is a seven-year-old's idea of sexy." **5** W. Phillips, "Poppy the Populist," *Newsweek*, 7/11/88. "Bush has always seemed to consider campaigning a kind of slumming. That is why he turned to the likes of the late Lee Atwater, who never found a tone he could not lower." —George Will, *Newsweek*, 2/10/92. **6** I: Donna Binder. **7** M: Eli Reed. 1,600,000 homeless U.S. children living in shelters, cars, abandoned buildings, campsites, etc. (The Alliance Committee). **8** W. William O. Douglas quoted by Harry Kalven, Jr., in *A Worthy Tradition*. "A different aesthetic is presumed to be no aesthetic. And the female, black, working-class or homosexual experience is uncritically assumed to be, at best, an unlikely candidate for canonization, precisely because it is the marked variant, whereas the experience of straight, white men has a unique claim to universality." —Lillian S. Robinson, *The Nation*, 9/25/89. Robert Mapplethorpe (1946–1989) died of AIDS. **9** Margaret Morton. ". . . the need to personalize the living environment goes far beyond the need for mere shelter, no matter how extreme the circumstances." —Morton, "The Architecture of Despair." **10, 12** I: Kirk Condyles, Meredith McCroyd. **11** Elizabeth Glasgow. More than 50% of Americans trace their roots through Ellis Island. **13** W. **14, 16** I: Kirk Condyles. **15** I: Dana Schuerholz. 15% of old-growth U.S. forests remain; at the current cutting rate of 170 acres daily, all virgin woodland will be gone in 15 years. **17** I: Cindy Reiman. **18** M: Paul Fusco. Michael Ventura, *LA Weekly*, 3/15/91. 11 million gallons were spilled. Exxon pleaded guilty, but when a federal judge rejected a proposed settlement of $1 billion plus $100 million in criminal charges as insufficient for the huge task of cleaning it up, Exxon withdrew its guilty plea and dug in for a prolonged court battle. **19** U. The quake, 6.9 on the Richter scale and lasting 15 seconds, hit San Francisco, Santa Cruz, and Oakland, where the upper deck of the interstate collapsed, trapping 40 people in their cars. **20** W. The total meltdown at the U.S.S.R.'s Chernobyl plant in 1986 left 1 million "at risk" over 13,000 square miles. Children are 100 times more susceptible to radiation poisoning than are adults. **21** M: James Nachtway. Romania's Ceausescu bought contaminated blood on the international blood market and sold it to state hospitals, instituting a policy of giving transfusions to infants. **22** W. "From the first moment, the embassy worked to minimize the costs of the massacre for the armed forces. The American Embassy lied, contradicted itself, and even placed people's lives in danger."—Fr. Jose Tojeira, Jesuit Provincial for Central America. "The killers of the Jesuits did more harm to U.S. policy in El Salvador and to the armed forces than any damage by the FMLN." —William Walker, U.S. Ambassador to El Salvador. **23** Jim Tynan. **24, 25** W. **26** U. **27** W. **28** Alberto L. Muschette. **29** U. **30** G. **31, 33** W. **32** M: Leonard Freed. **34** I: Stig Stassig. "What do we have to do for you Americans to do something in return? Restore the Romanovs to the throne?" —Mikhail Gorbachev. **35** U. "Can we recover the memory of what we were before we became what we are now?" —Senator Patrick Moynihan, "End of the Cold War Act 1991." DIVERSIONS: **36, 38, 52** W. Over the years, Charles Keating contributed $1.3 million to campaigns of or groups supported by five senators: Alan Cranston, Dennis DeConcini, John Glen, John McCain, and Donald Riegle. They intervened with federal regulators, adding as much as $1.3 billion to the total bailout bill of $2.5 billion for Lincoln S&L. **37, 46, 48, 50, 51** U. The cost of Reagan's visit to Japan ($2 million) got him some bad press; his personal fortune of $4 million, one year after leaving the presidency, rose to $10 million. **42** Angelika Films. **43** G. **44** Ann Fuller. **47** NASA. **45** Camera Wide. **49** Sharon Smith. OBITS: **53, 55, 56, 57, 60, 61, 62, 64, 69, 70** W. **58, 63, 66, 68** U. **59** L. **71** Philip-Lorca diCorcia.

TERRORISTS TO REASON

All photos: W. **4.** Though Doe, a Cold War asset, received $500 million in U.S. aid between 1980 and 1985, 80% of Liberia's population is illiterate and its health statistics are among the world's worst. **5.** Duke, elected to the Louisiana state legislature with 78% of the vote, said: "I feel...comfortable in the Republican Party." **6.** "The French clearly found the cause of AIDS first and Dr. Gallo clearly tried to upstage them one year later." —Dr. Don Francis, Centers for Disease Control. **8, 11.** "During '81, '82, and '83, top-level officials of the EPA violated their public trust by disregarding the public health and the environment, manipulating the Superfund program for political purposes, engaging in unethical conduct, and participating in other abuses." —U.S. House of Representatives Energy and Commerce Oversight Subcommittee. **10.** The Laffer Curve made visible the theory of "trickle-down" economics. **13.** After the CIA-backed assassination of Lumumba in 1965, Mobutu, a Cold War asset, came to power; his personal fortune is estimated at $5 billion in a country where 33⅓% of the children die of malnutrition before age five. **15.** "Silent Sam" Pierce, a former Wall Street lawyer, took the Fifth before the congressional committee set up to examine HUD's billions in losses. A 1986 audit disclosed that 16 out of 17 projects failed to create inexpensive housing. **16.** "Democracy is the breeding ground of communism." —Augusto Pinochet, who rose to power after the 1973 CIA-backed assassination of president-elect Allende. **17.** With his crony Son Sen, Pol Pot was responsible for the murder of more than 1 million Cambodians. **18.** St. Germain was cosponsor of the S&L deregulation bill, and a most-favored recipient of Thrift's PAC money. He lost his House seat of 28 years while the Ethics Committee was investigating his numerous conflicts of interest. **19.** "[Shad] threw out SEC regulations that he considered duplicative and expensive for companies.... Without the SEC peering as closely over their shoulders, some of the biggest investment firms witnessed a breakdown in discipline among their stockbrokers, especially in the area of fraudulent sales practices." —David A. Vise and Steve Coll, *Washington Post.* **24.** Waldheim's Nazi past did not prevent him from being elected. **25.** In 1987, CIA "coup maker" Vernon Walters organized the overthrow of elected prime minister Bavadra who had declared Fiji a nuclear-free zone. **26.** When Vice President Bush praised Zia for his antinarcotics program in 1984, Pakistan was supplying 70% of the world's heroin and was the fifth largest recipient of U.S. aid.

HEARTS OF THE EIGHTIES

1, 2 U. **3** Anders Goldfarb. **4, 5** W. When New Zealand outlawed nuclear weapons in its port, the U.S. threatened to withdraw from the Anzus pact. "I regard it as unacceptable that another country should by threat or coercion try to change a policy that has been embraced by the New Zealand people." —David Lange. **6, 7, 8, 9, 10, 11, 12, 13, 14** W.

STILL GOING STRONG

1, 2, 3, 4, 5, 6 W. "Our polity is now the least informed in the industrial world, and Europeans are starting to tell American jokes every bit as disagreeable as our Polish jokes." —Gore Vidal. **7** W. "The Caesars weren't tyrannical. They were guys who wanted to be loved, like the president. But they exercised power unrestrained by a Constitution, like the president." —Representative Henry B. Gonzalez, Texas. **8, 10, 11, 12, 13** W.